MEDITERRANEAN DIET
COOKBOOK FOR BEGINNERS

Easy and Tasty Recipes, 27 Days of Meal Plans to Help you Lose Weight and Burn Fat.

OLIVIA MARINI

Table of Contents

Sommario

INTRODUCTION   **5**

WHAT YOU SHOULD KNOW ABOUT THE MEDITERRANEAN DIET   **7**

   MEDITERRANEAN NUTRITION PYRAMID   7

   PROS OF THE MEDITERRANEAN DIET FOR YOUR HEALTH   7

   FOOD TO EAT: KIND   8

   LIST OF FOODS FOR THE MEDITERRANEAN DIET   9

BREAKFAST RECIPES   **14**

   Feta - Avocado & Mashed Chickpea Toast   14

   Mango Pear Smoothie   14

   Mediterranean Smoothie   15

   Fruit Smoothie   15

   Strawberry-Rhubarb Smoothie   15

   Chia-Pomegranate Smoothie   16

   Egg White Scramble with Cherry Tomatoes & Spinach   16

   Blueberry, Hazelnut, and Lemon Breakfast Grain Salad   17

   Blueberry Greek Yogurt Pancakes   18

   Pastry-Less Spanakopita   19

   Date and Walnut Overnight Oats   20

   Pear and Mango Smoothie   20

BREADS, RICE, AND PASTA RECIPE BOOK   **22**

   15 Minute Caprese Pasta Recipe   22

   Mediterranean One Pot Pasta   23

   Farfalle With Tuna, Lemon, And Fennel   24

   Easy Italian Shrimp Tortellini Bake   24

   Pasta Fagioli   25

   Sweet Potato Noodles with Almond Sauce   26

   Shrimp And Pasta Stew   27

   Cold Lemon Zoodles   28

   Pasta Alla Norma with Eggplant, Basil & Pecorino   29

   Tortellini With Pesto & Broccoli   30

   Spinach Pesto Pasta   31

   Authentic Pasta e Fagioli   31

Chicken Spinach and Artichoke Stuffed Spaghetti Squash   32

Angel Hair with Asparagus-Kale Pesto   33

Spicy Pasta Puttanesca   34

PIZZA RECIPES   **36**

Shrimp Pizza   36

Veggie Pizza   36

Watermelon Feta & Balsamic Pizza   37

White Pizza with Prosciutto and Arugula   38

Za'atar Pizza   38

Pizza Dough On Yogurt   39

American Pizza Dough Recipe   39

Sprouts Pizza   40

Cheese Pinwheels   41

Ground Meat Pizza   41

MEAT: PORK, LAMB & BEEF RECIPES   **43**

Mediterranean Pork Kabobs   43

Mediterranean Meatball and Orzo Bowls   43

Mediterranean Pork Chops   45

Mediterranean Grilled Steak   45

Barbecue Bacon-Wrapped Shrimp with Basil Stuffing   46

Lebanese Meat Pies   47

Easy Mediterranean Burers   48

Mediterranean Pork Chop   50

Hummus With Spiced Beef and Toasted Pine Nuts   51

Spiced Beef and Lamb Kebabs   52

Stuffed Baby Eggplant with Spiced Ground Beef, Bulgur and Pine Nuts   54

FISH & SEAFOOD RECIPES   **56**

Grilled Salmon   56

Dijon Mustard and Lime Marinated Shrimp   56

Dill Relish on White Sea Bass   57

Sweet Potatoes Oven Fried   58

Tasty Avocado Sauce over Zoodles   58

Tomato Basil Cauliflower Rice   59

Vegan Sesame Tofu and Eggplants   59

Baked Sea Bass   60

Fish and Tomato Sauce 61

Seafood Paella 61

Escabeche 62

Crispy Sardines 63

Roasted Salmon 64

Almond-Crusted Swordfish 65

Lemon Rosemary Branzino 66

Black Bean Pasta 67

Fish Tacos 67

Grilled Tilapia with Mango Salsa 68

DESSERT RECIPES **70**

Almond Cookies 70

Crunchy Sesame Cookies 70

Mini Orange Tarts 71

Traditional Kalo Prama 71

Turkish-Style Chocolate Halva 72

SPECIAL RECIPES IN 15 MINUTES **74**

Beef and Broccoli Stir-Fry 74

Parmesan-Crusted Halibut with Asparagus 74

Hearty Beef and Bacon Casserole 75

Baked Zucchini Noodles with Feta 76

SPECIAL VEGAN RECIPES **78**

Garlic Mushrooms 78

Rosemary Potatoes 78

Roasted Spicy Carrots 79

Baked Artichoke Fries 79

Baked Tofu Strips 80

SPECIAL VEGETARIAN RECIPES **81**

Lemon Broccoli Rabe 81

Spicy Swiss Chard 81

Roasted Almond Protein Salad 82

Black-Eyed Pea, Beet, and Carrot Stew 83

Koshari 83

SPECIAL GLUTEN RECIPES **85**

Blueberries Quinoa 85

Raspberries and Yogurt Smoothie   85

Cottage Cheese and Berries Omelet   85

Salmon Frittata   86

Avocado and Olive Paste on Toasted Rye Bread   86

SALAD   **88**

Brown Rice Salad with Pistachios and Basil   88

Spinach and Avocado Salad   89

Mixed Salad with Balsamic Honey Dressing   89

Arugula and Fig Salad   90

Arugula, Watermelon, and Feta Salad   90

Green Bean and Halloumi Salad   91

Citrus Salad with Kale and Fennel   92

Cauliflower Tabbouleh Salad   93

27 DAY PLAN (DETOX-FOOD BALANCE-LOSE WEIGHT)   **94**

CONCLUSION   **98**

WOW BONUS   **99**

Basic Conversion Charts   **100**

Cooking Measurement Conversion Chart   101

INTRODUCTION

The countries that sit on the coast of the Mediterranean Sea are responsible for developing this high-nutrient, plant-based diet. The traditional or healthy Mediterranean diet is the result of the long-standing dietary practices of these countries. Fruits, vegetables, and whole grains (like pasta and bread) make up the bulk of this diet, with moderate amounts of fish and minimal to moderate amounts of red meat rounding out the list of food groups. People who are concerned with maintaining a healthy weight and an active lifestyle continue to place a premium on following traditional eating patterns. This diet based on foods from the Mediterranean has been examined extensively over the past 20 years. It has been demonstrated to improve cardiovascular health, lower blood sugar in diabetics, aid in cholesterol management, and lessen the likelihood of developing osteoporosis, cancer, and Alzheimer's disease.

See how the different food groups can be balanced in the Mediterranean diet pyramid below. Breads and grains form the base of the pyramid, followed by produce. Since dairy products are a good source of calcium, they are included. It's followed by things like fish, chicken, and nuts. Oils and fats, such as extra-virgin olive oil and nuts, are at the top.

Dietary Items Common to the Mediterranean Region: Fruits, including grapes: Berries: Produce of the earth, both fruitful and vegetable-like

Legumes/beans/pulses: Snacks like nuts, seeds, and nut butters: Oils/fats/butter/lard/ghee: There's a lot of flavor in tea, coffee, cocoa, and spices. Culinary seasonings and herbs.

A relatively small group of people from countries like Greece, Italy, and Spain are credited with spreading the idea of a Mediterranean diet. By the end of the 1700s, their developed cuisine was flourishing. The first decade of the twentieth century saw a large influx of Europeans to the United States, many of whom brought with them their wholesome ways of living. Greeks, Italians, and Spaniards who had emigrated to the Americas and missed their traditional Mediterranean diets were the first to adopt the diet. The diet has been adopted by many Americans, some of whom have even created their own versions on it.

Making the decision to adopt a healthier lifestyle is one thing, but really doing so is another. There are a lot of helpful tools and recommendations out there if you want to enhance your nutrition. Consider the information in this article as a jumping-off point for planning your next move.

An early version of the Mediterranean diet wasn't conceived as an all-encompassing lifestyle. Because people from places like Spain and Italy were already eating well before they relocated, they adopted more varied diets while still adhering to their cultural eating practices. Incorporating these older practices into the newer ones helped them meet their nutritional and aesthetic objectives. The people who lived in what is now Spain and Italy had access to a larger food supply and thus a higher standard of living because they could now purchase nutritious food.

People from the Mediterranean diaspora who settled in the Americas and the United States maintained their traditional dietary patterns even as their numbers grew. To further ensure the continued health and attractiveness of their new lifestyle, they took sure to keep their old practices apart from their new ones.

The word "Mediterranean" has recently gained in popularity. The term "Mediterranean diet" is frequently used, yet few Americans have a firm grasp on its meaning.

This book is designed for over 1200 days, as you can enjoy mixing and replicating the recipes presented with all your imagination for well beyond the next thousand days!

WHAT YOU SHOULD KNOW ABOUT THE MEDITERRANEAN DIET

MEDITERRANEAN NUTRITION PYRAMID

To help you better adhere to the guidelines of the Mediterranean Diet, here is an updated version of the traditional food pyramid. It specifies the types and amounts of food that should be eaten on a regular basis, monthly, weekly, and sometimes.

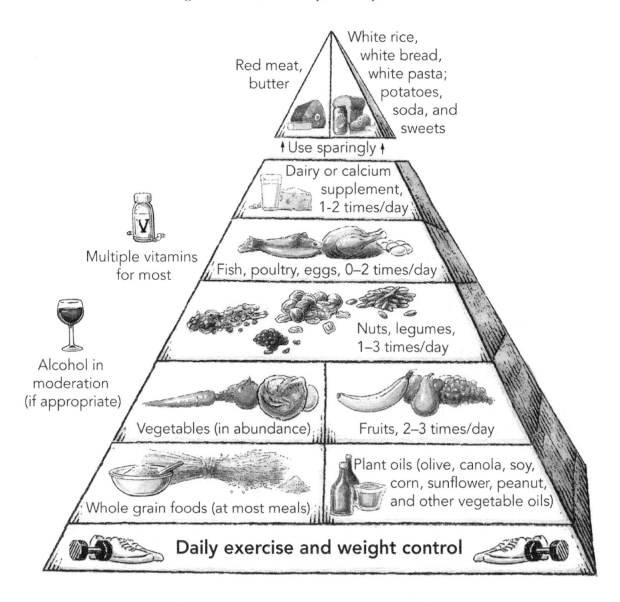

PROS OF THE MEDITERRANEAN DIET FOR YOUR HEALTH

Following are some of the benefits of the Mediterranean diet, as outlined by the National Institutes of Health:

- Consuming a diet rich in colorful fruits and vegetables and low in saturated fat, Trans fat, and cholesterol. The outcome is a diet rich in healthy options.

- A nutritious diet may help one achieve optimal health in many ways, including improved health indicators like lower blood pressure and cholesterol levels.
- Eating well can help improve cardiovascular health by lowering the likelihood of developing atherosclerosis and subsequent cardiovascular events like heart attacks and strokes. Keeping your blood pressure in the normal range is an important step in protecting your heart's health.
- Diets are commonly used as a means of weight loss and maintenance (in addition to regular exercise and healthy lifestyle habits).
- Nutrient-rich foods that promote longevity
- Maintaining a normal body weight, not smoking, and limiting one's exposure to harmful substances are all important factors in promoting healthy aging.
- Changing your diet to combat high blood pressure, estrogen dominance after menopause, and obesity will help lower your risk of developing endometrial cancer.
- To have a healthy pregnancy and lower the chance of miscarriage due to nutritional deficiencies, one should eat well.
- Dietary adjustments can reduce the risk of getting breast cancer by lowering risk factors such as obesity.

FOOD TO EAT: KIND

There are two main groups of foods that are considered suitable on the Mediterranean diet. You should eat moderate amounts of certain foods on a regular basis while limiting your intake of others. The following is a brief synopsis of the two classes.

Options for regularly consuming meals
- Extra-virgin olive oil, avocado oil, avocados, and olives are all examples of foods and oils that are both healthy and nutritious.
- Natural products include things like: peaches, figs, melons, dates, bananas, strawberries, grapes, pears, oranges, and apples. It's important to remember that this eating plan permits you to eat mainly whole, natural foods.
- Included in the category of vegetables are: cucumbers, Brussels sprouts, artichoke hearts, eggplants, carrots, cauliflower, onions, spinach, kale, broccoli, and tomatoes. These are only a few examples; in fact, almost any vegetable is fine on the Mediterranean diet.
- Pasta, whole wheat, full grain bread, corn, buckwheat, grain, rye, earth-toned rice, and whole oats are all examples of whole grains.
- Tubers and tuber-like plants, like potatoes, yams, turnips, and sweet potatoes.
- Chickpeas, peanuts, buckwheat, lentils, peas, and beans are all great sources of protein and fiber.

- Fish, in particular, provides a substantial portion of the daily protein requirement. Crab, mussels, clams, shrimp, fish, haddock, and salmon are just some of the authentic shellfish featured in these models.
- Consume all foods in moderation.
- The foods listed below are probably less healthy options than the food groups already mentioned.
- Bacon, ground beef, and steak are all examples of carcasses.
- Low-fat or fat-free milk, yogurt, and cheese. Cheese, yogurt, and low-fat milk are just a few examples of well-known dairy products.
- Poached or cooked eggs, which may be an excellent protein source.
- Wild birds, quail, and chickens
- Remember that skinless chickens are just as nutritious as their skinless counterparts. For the obvious reason that doing so lowers cholesterol levels in the chicken.
- This list of foods is expanded upon later in the book so that you know what foods to eat on a daily, weekly, and monthly basis while following a Mediterranean diet.

The kinds of foods to avoid
- Below is a list of foods that are not allowed on the Mediterranean diet. It's because they're unlucky, and so denying you the benefits of a Mediterranean diet. Avoid processed meats like bacon, frankfurters, and wieners because to their high levels of dangerous saturated fats. Stay away from refined oils like cottonseed oil, vegetable oil, and soybean oil.
- Trans fats (also known as submerged fats), which can be found in spreads and margarine.
- Avoid eating foods that have been heavily processed. I'm referring to every single variety of processed food. This is a great way to sell perishable raw products like almonds, wheat, etc. Despite their low-fat labels, some of these foods are actually quite high in sugar.
- Avoid foods that are made with white flour, such as pasta, bread, cereal, bagels, and other similar goods.
- The added sugar in meals like soft drinks, chocolates, snacks, and frozen yogurt makes them unhealthy choices.

LIST OF FOODS FOR THE MEDITERRANEAN DIET

Mediterranean cooking techniques place an emphasis on using healthy cooking methods in order to realize the full health benefits of the Mediterranean diet. Following the below suggestions will help ensure that your next meal turns out delicious.
- Using a pressure cooker results in the largest loss of nutrients, according to a study published in the journal of food sciences nutrition; therefore, minimizing the amount of

time food spends in the oven is recommended. Get rid of the pressure cooker and replace it with some other method.

- Increase the oven temperature and decrease the baking time.
- Roasting and baking are the greatest methods of cooking meat and vegetables.
- The nutrients are more likely to survive in the sautéing process.
- Frying is fine and can even be beneficial because it locks in the food's natural moisture, but it's preferable to limit the number of times you reuse the oil.

To-Buy List:
When it comes to vegetables, it's best to stick to what's in season and within driving distance.

- Cucumbers
- Onions
- Tomatoes
- Eggplant
- Peppers

Foods:
- Lettuce Romaine
- Cabbage
- Mushrooms
- Peas
- Beets
- Cauliflower
- Celery
- Potatoes
- Carrots
- Zucchini
- Green Beans
- Broccoli
- Spinach

The citrus fruit is the most abundant source of antioxidants among fruits.

- Strawberry
- Peaches
- Lemon
- Pears
- Fig
- Cantaloupe

- Watermelon
- Cherry
- Apricot
- Apples
- Tangerine
- Oranges

Bread and other grains:
- Barley
- The pita
- Couscous
- Egg-based Pasta
- 100% whole wheat bread
- Rice
- Pasta
- Phyllo
- Bulgur
- Breadsticks

Dairy: Typically, full-fat dairy products are included in the Mediterranean diet.
- Yogurt made in Greece
- Fresh mozzarella
- Goat Cheese
- Lamb yogurt
- Feta cheese
- Mitzithra
- Grated Parmesan
- Gorgonzola cheese
- Ricotta Cheese
- Manchego cheese

Meat and poultry are weekly staples in most people's diets.
- Chicken
- Turkey
- Veal
- Pork
- Beef

- Game

Fatty, tiny fish are the mainstay of the seafood diet, and this includes canned goods.
- Cod
- Shrimps
- Octopus
- Calamari
- Sardines
- Anchovies

Spices and Herbs:
- Black Pepper
- Cinnamon
- Cumin
- Oregano
- Sage
- Parsley
- Dill
- Basil
- Kosher salt
- Thyme

Grocery Items:
- canned tomatoes
- Honey
- Capers
- Balsamic Vinegar
- Wine
- Vinegar of red wine
- Paste made of tomatoes
- Olives
- Tahini
- Unrefined, pure olive oil

So, spend the majority of your grocery budget on vegetables and fruits, less on fish, and the least on meat and dairy.

BREAKFAST RECIPES

Feta - Avocado & Mashed Chickpea Toast

Preparation Time: 10 minutes

Cooking Time: 15 minutes

Servings: 4

Ingredients:

- 15 ounces can Chickpeas
- 2 ounces - ½ cup diced feta cheese
- 1 pitted avocado
- Fresh juice:
- 2 teaspoons lemon (or 1 tablespoon orange)
- ½ teaspoon Black pepper
- 2 teaspoons honey
- 4 slices Multigrain toast

Direction

- Brown the bread in the toaster. The chickpeas should be drained in a colander. Put the avocado flesh in the bowl using a spoon. They should be mashed with a big fork or a potato masher until the mixture may be spreadable.
- Add the feta cheese, pepper, and lemon juice to the bowl. Combine, then spread evenly over each of the four pieces of bread. Honey should be drizzled over the dish before it is served.

Nutritional Value: Calories: 337 Carbs: 43 g Fat: 13 g Protein: 13 g

Mango Pear Smoothie

Preparation Time: 5 minutes

Cooking Time: 0 minute

Servings: 1

Ingredients:

- 2 ice cubes
- ½ cup Greek yogurt, plain
- ½ mango, peeled, pitted & chopped
- 1 cup kale, chopped
- 1 pear, ripe, cored & chopped

Direction

- Gather all of the components and put them into your mixer or blender. Combine and blend until completely smooth and creamy. Serve.

Nutritional Value: Calories 350 Protein 40 g Fats 12 g Carbohydrates: 11 g

Mediterranean Smoothie

Preparation Time: 5 minutes
Cooking Time: 5 minutes
Servings: 2
Ingredients:
- 2 cups of baby spinach
- 1 teaspoon fresh ginger root
- 1 frozen banana, pre-sliced
- 1 small mango
- ½ cup beet juice
- ½ cup of skim milk
- 4-6 ice cubes

Direction
- Gather all of the components and put them into your mixer or blender. Combine and blend until completely smooth and creamy. Serve.

Nutritional Value: Calories: 168 Protein: 4 g Fat: 1 g Carbohydrates: 39 g

Fruit Smoothie

Preparation Time: 5 minutes
Cooking Time: 0 minutes
Servings: 2
Ingredients:
- 2 cups blueberries (or any fresh or frozen fruit, cut into pieces if the fruit is large)
- 2 cups unsweetened almond milk
- 1 cup crushed ice
- ½ teaspoon ground ginger (or other dried ground spice such as turmeric, cinnamon, or nutmeg)

Direction
- Place the blueberries, almond milk, ice, and ginger in a blender and process until smooth. Combine until there are no lumps.

Nutritional Value: Calories: 125 Protein: 2 g Carbohydrates: 23 g Fat: 4 g

Strawberry-Rhubarb Smoothie

Preparation Time: 5 minutes
Cooking Time: 3 minutes

Servings: 1

Ingredients:

- 1 rhubarb stalk, chopped
- 1 cup sliced fresh strawberries
- ½ cup plain Greek yogurt
- 2 tablespoons honey
- Pinch ground cinnamon
- 3 ice cubes

Direction

- Over high heat, bring a small saucepan full of water to a boil in the saucepan. After adding the rhubarb, continue boiling for another three minutes. After draining the liquid, place the rhubarb in a blender.
- Put the strawberries, yogurt, honey, and cinnamon in a food processor and run it until the mixture is completely smooth. After adding the ice, continue blending until the mixture becomes thick and there are no ice chunks left. Pour the smoothie into a glass, and then consume it at room temperature.

Nutritional Value: Calories: 295 Fat: 8 g Carbohydrates: 56 g Protein: 6 g

Chia-Pomegranate Smoothie

Preparation Time: 5 minutes

Cooking Time: 0 minutes

Servings: 2

Ingredients:

- 1 cup pure pomegranate juice (no sugar added)
- 1 cup frozen berries
- 1 cup coarsely chopped kale
- 2 tablespoons chia seeds
- 3 Medjool dates, pitted and coarsely chopped
- Pinch ground cinnamon

Direction

- Place the pomegranate juice, berries, and kale in a blender along with the chia seeds, dates, and cinnamon. Pulse the mixture until it is completely smooth. Pour into glasses, then proceed with serving.

Nutritional Value: Calories: 275 Fat: 5 g Carbohydrates: 59 g Protein: 5 g

Egg White Scramble with Cherry Tomatoes & Spinach

Preparation Time: 5 minutes

Cooking Time: 8-10 minutes

Servings: 4

Ingredients:

- 1 tablespoon olive oil
- 1 whole egg
- 10 white eggs
- ¼ teaspoon black pepper
- ½ teaspoon salt
- 1 garlic clove, minced
- 2 cups cherry tomatoes, halved
- 2 cups packed fresh baby spinach
- ½ cup light cream or Half & Half
- ¼ cup finely grated parmesan cheese

Direction

- Whisk the eggs, pepper, salt, and milk. Make ready to use a skillet by heating it to a temperature of medium-high. When the skillet is heated, throw in the garlic and allow it to sauté for about a quarter of a minute.
- After adding the tomatoes and spinach, continue to sauté the mixture for one more minute after adding them. It is best if the tomatoes are allowed to become more pliable and the spinach is allowed to wilt.
- While the pan is on a heat setting of medium, add the egg mixture to the pan. While it cooks for around two to three minutes, carefully fold the egg while it is cooking. Remove from the heat source, and top with a little dusting of grated cheese.
  Nutritional Value: Calories 142 Protein: 15 g Fat: 2 g Carbs 4 g

Blueberry, Hazelnut, and Lemon Breakfast Grain Salad

Preparation Time: 5 minutes

Cooking Time: 10 minutes

Servings: 8

Ingredients:

- 1 cup steel-cut oats
- 1 cup dry golden quinoa
- ½ cup dry millet
- 3 tablespoons olive oil, divided
- ¾ teaspoon salt
- 1 x 1" piece fresh ginger, peeled and cut into coins
- 2 large lemons, zest and juice

- ½ cup maple syrup
- 1 cup Greek yogurt
- ¼ tsp nutmeg
- 2 cups hazelnuts, roughly chopped and toasted
- 2 cups blueberries or mixed berries
- 4½ cups water

Direction

- Get a strainer with a mesh top and put the oats, quinoa, and millet in it. After a thorough cleaning, set it to the side. Find a saucepan with a capacity of three quarts, pour one tablespoon of oil into it, and place the pan on the stove over medium heat.
- After toasting for a couple of minutes, add the grains to the pan. Add the water, salt, ginger coins, and lemon zest to the bowl and stir to combine. Bring to a boil, then immediately cover and reduce the heat to a simmer. Maintain a low simmer for twenty minutes.
- Remove from the heat and let stand for five minutes before serving. After removing the ginger and fluffing the rice with a fork, set it aside to cool for at least an hour. Get yourself a big bowl and put the grains in it.
- Grab a bowl that's about the size of a medium and add the rest of the olive oil, the lemon juice, the maple syrup, the yogurt, and the nutmeg. Combine everything by giving it a thorough whisking. After pouring it over the grains, thoroughly mix it.
- After adding the hazelnuts and blueberries, give the mixture another toss and place it in the refrigerator for the night. Serve and enjoy.

Nutritional Value: Calories 363 Fat: 11 g Carbs: 60 g Protein: 7 g

Blueberry Greek Yogurt Pancakes

Preparation Time: 15 minutes
Cooking Time: 15 minutes
Servings: 6

Ingredients:

- 1¼ cup all-purpose flour
- 2 teaspoons baking powder
- 1 teaspoon baking soda
- ¼ teaspoon salt
- ¼ cup sugar
- 3 eggs
- 3 tablespoons vegan butter unsalted, melted
- ½ cup milk
- 1½ cups Greek yogurt plain, non-fat

- ½ cup blueberries optional

Toppings:

- Greek yogurt
- Mixed berries – blueberries, raspberries and blackberries

Direction

- Put the flour, salt, baking powder, and baking soda into a large basin and mix them together with a whisk. In a separate dish, combine butter, sugar, eggs, Greek yogurt, and milk, and whisk all of the ingredients together until creamy.
- After that, add the Greek yogurt mixture from step 1 to the dry ingredients from step 1, mix until combined, and then leave the batter to sit for 20 minutes to create a smooth texture. If you are using blueberries, fold them into the pancake batter.
- While the griddle for the pancakes is heating up, brush it with butter or spray it with a non-stick butter spray. The batter should be poured onto the griddle in increments of a quarter cup.
- Continue cooking until the bubbles on the surface of the pancakes break and make little holes; then, raise the corners of the pancakes to check whether or not the bottoms are golden brown.
- Turn the pancake over with a wide spatula, and continue cooking on the other side until it is gently browned. Serve.

Nutritional Value: Calories: 258 Carbohydrates: 33 g Fat: 8 g Protein: 11 g

Pastry-Less Spanakopita

Preparation Time: 5 minutes

Cooking Time: 20 minutes

Servings: 4

Ingredients:

- 1/8 teaspoons black pepper, add as per taste
- 1/3 cup of Extra-virgin olive oil
- 4 lightly beaten eggs
- 7 cups of Lettuce, preferably a spring mix (mesclun)
- ½ cup of crumbled Feta cheese
- 1/8 teaspoon of Sea salt, add to taste
- 1 finely chopped medium yellow onion

Direction

- Preheat the oven to 180 degrees Celsius and oil the tart pan. When you are finished, transfer the onions to a big saucepan, add the extra-virgin olive oil, and cook them together over a medium heat until the onions become translucent.

- After adding the greens, continue to stir the mixture until all of the ingredients have been wilted. After seasoning it with salt and pepper, move the greens to the plate that has been prepared, and then add some feta cheese on top of the greens.
- Pour in the eggs, then place in the oven for 20 minutes, or until it is golden and completely cooked through.
  Nutritional Value: Calories: 325 Protein: 11.2 g Fat: 27.9 g Carbs: 7.3 g

Date and Walnut Overnight Oats

Preparation Time: 5 minutes
Cooking Time: 20 minutes
Servings: 2
Ingredients:
- ¼ cup Greek yogurt, plain
- 1/3 cup of yogurt
- 2/3 cup of oats
- 1 cup of milk
- 2 teaspoons date syrup or you can also use maple syrup or honey
- 1 mashed banana
- ¼ teaspoon cinnamon
- ¼ cup walnuts
- pinch of salt (approx.1/8 teaspoon)
  Direction
- To begin, obtain a Mason jar or a small bowl and pour all of the ingredients into either one of these containers. After that, give all of the components a thorough swirl and blend. It should be cooled overnight in the refrigerator after being properly covered and secured.
- After that, take it out the following morning, and if necessary, add additional liquid or cinnamon, and then serve it chilled. (However, you may alternatively heat it in the microwave for those who want a more robust flavor.)
  Nutritional Value: Calories: 350 Protein: 14 g Fat: 12 g Carbs: 49 g

Pear and Mango Smoothie

Preparation Time: 5 minutes
Cooking Time: 0 minutes
Servings: 1
Ingredients:
- 1 ripe mango, cored and chopped

- ½ mango, peeled, pitted and chopped
- 1 cup kale, chopped
- ½ cup plain Greek yogurt
- 2 ice cubes

Direction

- Place the pear, mango, yogurt, kale, and mango in a blender and process until smooth. After adding ice, combine the mixture until it has a smooth consistency. Serve, and have fun with it!

Nutritional Value: Calories: 293 Fat: 8 g Carbohydrates: 53 g Protein: 8 g

BREADS, RICE, AND PASTA RECIPE BOOK

15 Minute Caprese Pasta Recipe

Preparation time: 5 minutes

Cooking time: 10 minutes

Servings: 4

Ingredients:

- 1-pound Angel Hair Pasta
- 4 tablespoons Olive Oil
- 1 small Onion, finely chopped
- 4 cloves Garlic, finely minced
- 3 cups Cherry Tomatoes, quartered
- 2 handfuls Fresh Basil, large, thinly sliced
- 8 ounces Mozzarella Cheese, sliced into small cubes
- 1 tablespoon Balsamic Vinegar, optional
- salt and freshly ground black pepper, to taste
- Crushed Red Pepper Flakes, optional
- Grated Parmesan Cheese, to serve

Direction

- Place a generous amount of salt in a large pot and bring it to a boil along with the water. When cooking the pasta, make sure to follow the recommendations on the package. Drain, making sure to set aside a half a cup of the cooking liquid.
- In the time it takes for the pasta to cook, prepare the following: One tablespoon of olive oil should be heated up over medium heat in a big pan. The onion and the garlic should be cooked for three minutes, or until the onion has softened.
- Toss the spaghetti with the remaining ingredients, which are as follows:
- While the pan is heating up, toss the spaghetti with the sauce in the pan until it is completely covered.
- After one more minute has passed, toss the tomatoes into the pan with the remaining three tablespoons of olive oil.
- To maintain its moistness, add a couple of tablespoons of the boiling water that the pasta was cooked in.
- Add basil, mozzarella, and balsamic vinegar to taste, then season with salt and pepper (if using).
- Serve at once, topping each portion with grated parmesan cheese.

Nutritional Value: Calories: 433 kcal, Protein 47 grams, Carbs: 55 grams, Fat: 15 grams

Mediterranean One Pot Pasta

Preparation Time: 10 minutes

Cooking Time: 15 minutes

Servings: 4

Ingredients:

- 1/8-ounce gluten free pasta corn/quinoa or chickpea/lentil*
- 3 cups water boiling
- 1 can vegetable broth
- 1 can fire roasted tomatoes
- 1 can artichoke hearts drained
- 1 cup black olives
- 1/2 purple onion sliced
- 2 tablespoons fresh thyme sub 1 teaspoon dried thyme
- 1 teaspoon cumin
- sea salt and black pepper to taste
- parmesan to serve, optional
- basil to serve, optional

Direction

- Start by bringing three cups of water to a boil in a large pot. In a large mixing bowl, combine the pasta with the vegetable broth, the onions, the tomatoes, the artichoke hearts, the olives, the thyme, and the cumin.
- Place the spaghetti in a large pot, place the pot over high heat, and toss the pasta often while it is cooking.
- Make sure the water continues to boil for the pasta, but reduce the temperature gradually while it cooks. To prevent the pasta from clumping together or adhering to the bottom of the pot, use the tongs to give it a toss at regular intervals.
- Maintain constant vigilance over the pasta until the water evaporates and the sauce develops. In the event that the pasta requires more cooking time, dilute the sauce by gradually adding half a cup of hot water at a time.
- After the sauce has decreased in volume, season it with salt and pepper.
- Remove the pasta from the skillet and immediately place it on individual plates in order to prevent the pasta from being overcooked in the liquid.
- Place on a serving platter right away and top with freshly chopped herbs or grated parmesan cheese.

Nutritional Value: Calories: 489 kcal, Protein 65 grams, Carbs: 42 grams, Fat: 35 grams

Farfalle With Tuna, Lemon, And Fennel

Preparation time: 10 minutes

Cooking time: 20 minutes

Servings: 4

Ingredients:

- 6 ounces dried whole grain farfalle (bow-tie) pasta
- 1 (5 ounce) can solid white tuna (packed in oil)
- 1 Olive oil
- 1 cup fennel, thinly sliced (1 medium bulb)
- 2 cloves garlic, minced
- ½ teaspoon crushed red pepper
- ¼ teaspoon salt
- 2 (14.5 ounce) cans no-salt-added diced tomatoes, undrained
- 2 tablespoons snipped fresh Italian (flat leaf) parsley
- 1 teaspoon lemon peel, finely shredded

Direction

- Drain the pasta and boil it according to the directions on the package, but do not add any salt. Place the spaghetti back in the pan and cover it so that it will remain warm. In the meantime, drain the can of tuna and set the oil aside. If necessary, add an additional tablespoon of olive oil to get the total up to three. Set aside flakes of tuna.

- Three teaspoons of oil that has been preserved, heated in a medium skillet over medium heat Fennel should be cooked for three minutes while being stirred at regular intervals. Continue to stir while cooking for one minute, or until the garlic becomes golden.

- The tomatoes are added at the very end. Bring to a boil, then remove from the heat immediately. Cover and continue cooking for five to six minutes, or until the mixture has reached the desired consistency. After the tuna has been thoroughly cooked, stir it in and continue cooking for another minute or two with the lid off.

- Place the pasta in a large bowl and pour the tuna mixture over it. Toss to combine. On top of each dish, some grated lemon peel and chopped parsley should be sprinkled.
  Nutritional Value: Calories: 442 kcal | Protein 54 grams | Carbs: 66 grams | Fat: 21 grams

Easy Italian Shrimp Tortellini Bake

Preparation time: 15 minutes

Cooking time: 5 minutes

Servings: 6

Ingredients:

- 3/4 lb. jumbo shrimp, peeled and deveined

- 2 9oz packages of whole wheat cheese tortellini (use regular if you're not a fan of whole wheat)
- 2 - 2 1/2 c marinara or spaghetti sauce
- 1/2 - 3/4 c shredded mozzarella cheese
- 1.5 tbsp parmesan cheese
- 2 tbsp extra virgin olive oil
- Salt and pepper to taste
- Fresh chopped parsley for garnish

Direction

- Set the broiler to its highest setting.
- After heating the tortellini in accordance with the instructions on the package, place it in a separate bowl. After seasoning the shrimp with salt and pepper, toss them in olive oil and set them aside. Cook for three to five minutes on each side in a skillet that is suitable for the oven over medium heat, or until the meat becomes pink. Take the pan away from the fire and put it somewhere else. You are through using the stove, therefore you should turn it off now that you've reached this point.
- Transfer the cooked tortellini to the pan and stir them with the marinara sauce before adding them. On top of the shrimp, sprinkling some parmesan cheese and then some mozzarella cheese can't go wrong.
- Place under the broiler and cook until the cheese is golden brown and bubbling.

Nutritional Value: Calories: 573 kcal | Protein 55 grams | Carbs: 65 grams | Fat: 40 grams

Pasta Fagioli

Preparation time: 10 mins
Cooking time: 35 mins
Servings: 6

Ingredients:

- 2 tablespoons olive oil
- 1 small yellow onion chopped
- 1 medium carrot chopped
- 1 celery stalk chopped
- 3 cloves garlic minced
- 2 bay leaves
- 3 (15 oz) cans diced tomatoes
- 2 (14.5 oz) cans vegetable broth
- 2 (14 oz) cans cannellini beans, rinsed and drained

- 1 small parmesan rind
- 1 teaspoon dried thyme
- 1 teaspoon dried basil
- 1/2 teaspoon dried rosemary
- Dash of crushed red pepper
- 1 cup dried ditalini or other small pasta
- 1/4 cup chopped flat-leaf parsley
- Grated Parmesan cheese for servings, optional

Direction

- Place the olive oil in a large saucepan and bring it up to temperature over medium-high heat. After adding the onion, carrot, and celery, continue to simmer for another 5 minutes, or until the vegetables have become softer. After adding the garlic, continue cooking for another two minutes. Mix everything thoroughly after adding the bay leaves.
- In a large mixing bowl, combine the diced tomatoes, vegetable broth, beans, and the rind of the parmesan cheese. In a mixing dish, combine the thyme, basil, rosemary, and crushed red pepper. To taste, salt and black pepper is recommended. Allow the liquid to simmer on low heat for fifteen minutes.
- Raise the temperature to medium and add the pasta while stirring constantly. Cook for eight to ten minutes, stirring occasionally, or until the pasta is done. Add the parsley and combine everything thoroughly. Take the bay leaves out of the parmesan cheese, and peel the cheese.
- Serve in individual servings and, if desired, sprinkle grated Parmesan cheese on top.
Nutritional Value: Calories: 241 kcal | Protein 37 grams | Carbs: 33 grams | Fat: 21 grams

Sweet Potato Noodles with Almond Sauce

Preparation Time: 5 minutes
Cooking Time: 15 minutes
Servings: 4
Ingredients:
Almond Sauce:

- 2 tablespoons extra-virgin olive oil
- 3 shallots, minced
- 2 garlic cloves, minced
- 3 tablespoons all-purpose flour
- 2 cups plain, unsweetened almond milk
- 2 tablespoons Dijon mustard
- Salt and freshly ground black pepper

Sweet Potato Noodles:

- 2 tablespoons extra-virgin olive oil
- 3 sweet potatoes, cut into noodles (made using a spiralizer)
- 4 cups roughly torn kale
- Salt and freshly ground black pepper
- ½ cup toasted, salted almonds, roughly chopped

Direction

- Prepare the almond sauce by combining:
- Bring the olive oil to a simmer in a pot of medium size set over a medium heat. Shallots and garlic should be sautéed for one minute, or until the scent is released.
- After adding the flour, continue cooking for one minute while stirring the mixture continuously. Continuously whisking in the almond milk is necessary to prevent lumps from forming in the sauce. Continuous stirring over a medium heat setting is required in order to bring the mixture to a simmer. Prepare on a low heat for around four to five minutes.
- After incorporating the Dijon mustard into the sauce using a whisk, season it with salt and pepper. While the noodles are cooking, keep the sauce covered and continue to keep it warm over a low heat.
- Make the noodles using the sweet potato:
- Over a medium heat, bring the olive oil to a simmer in a large sauté pan. After adding the sweet potato noodles, continue to cook them for about 5 to 6 minutes, tossing them occasionally, or until they are almost completely soft.
- Stir in the greens and cook it until it becomes wilted. Toss the noodles in the sauce and continue to do so until they are well coated.
- Just before serving, add the almonds and mix everything together thoroughly. Salt & pepper to taste. As soon as possible, serve.

Nutritional Value: Calories: 555 kcal | Protein 58 grams | Carbs: 54 grams | Fat: 35 grams

Shrimp And Pasta Stew

Preparation Time: 15 minutes
Cooking Time: 30 minutes
Servings: 6 to 8

Ingredients:

- 2 tablespoons extra-virgin olive oil
- 2 cups peeled pearl onions (frozen is fine)
- 3 celery stalks, chopped
- 3 garlic cloves, minced

- ½ cup white wine
- 1 tablespoon hot paprika
- Pinch cayenne pepper
- 2 tablespoons lemon zest
- Kosher salt
- Freshly ground black pepper
- One 28-ounce can crush tomatoes
- 4 cups seafood or vegetable broth
- 2½ cups pasta (see finishing touches)
- 1½ pounds shrimp, peeled and deveined
- 3 cups roughly chopped kale
- Lemon zest, for garnish
- Chopped fresh parsley, for garnish

Direction

- Place the olive oil in a large saucepan and bring it up to temperature over medium heat. The onions and celery should be sautéed for about 5 to 6 minutes, or until they are soft. Continue to cook for one more minute, or until the garlic acquires a fragrant quality.
- Add the wine to the pan, then reduce the heat to a simmer. Cook for another 6 to 7 minutes, or until approximately half of the liquid has been evaporated. Paprika, cayenne pepper, lemon zest, salt, and pepper to taste. Continue to simmer for an additional one to two minutes, or until the scent is released.
- Bring the pot back to a simmer, then stir in the tomato paste and broth. Mix in the pasta, then return the pot to a boil for five minutes, or until the pasta is getting close to being tender. Turn the heat down to low, add the shrimp and kale, and continue to simmer, stirring periodically, for another four to five minutes, or until the pasta is tender, the shrimp are cooked all the way through, and the kale has wilted.
- To serve, ladle the stew into individual serving plates and sprinkle each with little lemon zest and chopped parsley. Serve with bread that has a crispy crust.

Nutritional Value: Calories: 875 kcal | Protein 44 grams | Carbs: 56 grams | Fat: 25 grams

Cold Lemon Zoodles

Preparation Time: 20 minutes
Cooking Time: 0 minutes
Servings: 5

Ingredients:

- 1 lemon, zested and juiced
- ½ teaspoon Dijon mustard

- ½ teaspoon garlic powder
- 1/3 cup olive oil
- Salt and freshly ground black pepper
- 3 medium zucchinis, cut into noodles (using a gadget like this)
- 1 bunch radishes, thinly sliced
- 1 tablespoon chopped fresh thyme
  Direction
- In a small mixing bowl, combine the lemon zest, lemon juice, mustard, and garlic powder.
- While continuing to whisk, gradually drizzle in the olive oil. Salt & pepper to taste.
- Place the radishes and zucchini noodles in a large mixing bowl and toss them together. Toss the veggies in the dressing until they are completely covered by it.
- Top with chopped fresh thyme and serve as soon as possible.
  Nutritional Value: Calories: 754 kcal | Protein 57 grams | Carbs: 32 grams | Fat: 45 grams

Pasta Alla Norma with Eggplant, Basil & Pecorino

Preparation Time: 20 minutes
Cooking Time: 40 minutes
Servings: 4
Ingredients:
- 4 tablespoons extra-virgin olive oil
- 1 large eggplant, sliced into 1-inch strips
- Kosher salt and freshly ground black pepper
- 1 sweet onion, thinly sliced
- 3 garlic cloves, peeled and crushed
- One 28-ounce can crush tomatoes
- 1 teaspoon crushed red pepper flakes
- ¾ teaspoon dried oregano
- 1-pound bite-size dry pasta, like rigatoni or macaroni
- ¼ cup chopped fresh parsley
- ¼ cup chopped fresh basil
- ½ cup grated pecorino or ricotta salata cheese
  Direction
- Place a large sauté pan over medium heat and begin to warm the olive oil in the pan. Prepare the eggplant in stages, turning it frequently, until it is golden brown on both

sides. After removing it from the skillet, transfer the eggplant to a large serving plate. Salt and pepper can be added to taste as a seasoning.

- Put the onion in the same pan and sauté it for approximately four minutes, or until it is tender. After adding the garlic and continuing to simmer for another minute, the garlic should become aromatic.
- Add the tomatoes, and bring the mixture to a simmer. After the addition of the red pepper flakes and oregano, season the dish with salt and pepper. Keep the temperature at a simmer for 15 to 20 minutes, or until the flavor has greatly grown and become concentrated.
- While the sauce is simmering, bring a large pot of salted water to a boil over high heat in another large saucepan. After adding the pasta, continue cooking it in accordance with the instructions on the package. Completely drain the liquid.
- Combine the eggplant and spaghetti with the sauce in a large bowl. Add the parsley, basil, and pecorino or ricotta salata, and mix everything together until it is well incorporated.
  Nutritional Value: Calories: 675 kcal | Protein 85 grams | Carbs: 69 grams | Fat: 55 grams

Tortellini With Pesto & Broccoli

Preparation time: 5 minutes
Cooking time: 5 minutes
Servings: 2
Ingredients:

- 140g Tender stem broccoli, cut into short lengths
- 250g fresh tortellini
- 3 tbsp pesto (fresh if you can get it)
- 2 tbsp toasted pine nuts
- 1 tbsp balsamic vinegar
- 8 cherry tomatoes, halved
  Direction
- Start by bringing a large saucepan full of water to a rolling boil. Following adding the broccoli, bring the mixture to a simmer for two minutes, after which you should add the tortellini and continue cooking for another two minutes, or as directed on the package. After everything has been drained, it should be washed with cold water until it has reached the desired temperature, and then it should be dumped into a basin. In a medium-sized mixing bowl, combine the pine nuts, balsamic vinegar, and pesto. After adding the tomatoes, immediately place them in storage containers and move them to a cool location. Bring the salad to room temperature in the morning so that you can get the most out of the flavor that the tomatoes and pesto have to offer.

Nutritional Value: Calories: 876kcal | Protein 43 grams | Carbs: 51 grams | Fat: 32 grams

Spinach Pesto Pasta

Preparation Time: 10 minutes
Cooking Time: 10 minutes
Servings: 4

Ingredients:

- 8 oz whole-grain pasta
- 1/3 cup mozzarella cheese, grated
- 1/2 cup pesto
- 5 oz fresh spinach
- 1 3/4 cup water
- 8 oz mushrooms, chopped
- 1 tbsp olive oil
- Pepper
- Salt

Direction

- Pour oil into the instant pot's inner pot, then turn the pressure cooker to the sauté setting.
- Add mushrooms and continue cooking for another five minutes.
- Pour the water over the spaghetti and give it a good swirl.
- Place the cover on the saucepan, then turn the heat to high and cook for 5 minutes.
- Once done, remove pressure using fast release. Remove lid.
- Add the last of the ingredients and stir until combined.
  Nutritional Value: Calories 213 Fat 17.3 g Carbohydrates 9.5 g Sugar 4.5 g Protein 7.4 g Cholesterol 9

Authentic Pasta e Fagioli

Preparation Time: 6 minutes
Cooking Time: 15 minutes
Servings: 4

Ingredients:

- 2 tablespoons olive oil
- 1 teaspoon garlic, pressed
- 4 small-sized potatoes, peeled and diced
- 1 parsnip, chopped

- 1 carrot, chopped
- 1 celery rib, chopped
- 1 leek, chopped
- 1 (6-ounce) can tomato paste
- 4 cups water
- 2 vegetable bouillon cubes
- 8 ounces cannellini beans, soaked overnight
- 6 ounces elbow pasta
- 1/2 teaspoon oregano
- 1/2 teaspoon basil
- 1/2 teaspoon fennel seeds
- Sea salt, to taste
- 1/4 teaspoon freshly cracked black pepper
- 2 tablespoons Italian parsley, roughly chopped

Direction

- Start by preheating your Instant Pot by pressing the "Sauté" button. Garlic, potatoes, parsnips, carrots, celery, and leeks should be sautéed in oil that has been heated until they have become tender.
- At this point, include the tomato paste, the water, the bouillon cubes, the cannellini beans, the elbow pasta, the oregano, the basil, the fennel seeds, the freshly cracked black pepper, and the sea salt.
- Make sure the cover is secure. To prepare food manually, select the "Manual" option and set the timer for 9 minutes at High pressure. When the cooking process is finished, do a rapid pressure release, and then carefully remove the cover.
- Garnish with parsley that is both fresh and Italian. Bon appétit!

Nutritional Value: 486 Calories; 8.3g Fat; 95g Carbs; 12.4g Protein; 11.4g Sugars; 14.8g Fiber

Chicken Spinach and Artichoke Stuffed Spaghetti Squash

Preparation Time: 10 minutes.

Cooking Time: 23 minutes.

Servings: 4

Ingredients:

- 4 oz reduced-fat cream cheese, cubed and softened
- 1/4 tsp ground pepper
- 3 tbsp water
- 1/4 tsp salt

- Crushed red peppers
- 3 lb. spaghetti squash, halved lengthwise and seeded
- 1/2 cup shredded parmesan cheese
- 5 oz pack baby spinach
- 10 oz pack artichoke hearts, chopped
- Diced fresh basil

Direction

- Arrange the squash halves in a dish that is safe for the microwave with the sliced side facing upward. To the squash, add two tablespoons of water. Cook the meal without covering it for approximately 15 minutes when the microwave is set to high power. You might alternatively set the squash on a prepared baking sheet with a rim and bake it for 40 minutes at a temperature of 400 degrees Fahrenheit.
- Turn the heat on your stove to medium and lay a big skillet with 1 tablespoon of water on the surface of the burner. After adding the spinach to the pan, simmer it for approximately five minutes, stirring it occasionally, or until the vegetable has wilted. The spinach should be drained and then placed in a basin.
- Position the rack in the upper third of the oven, and then start preheating the broiler.
- Using a fork, remove the squash flesh from both halves of the shell and set it in a basin. In the bowl containing the squash, combine artichoke hearts, pepper, salt, cream cheese, and a quarter cup of parmesan. Combine thoroughly. Put the hollowed-out squash on a baking sheet, then spoon the squash mixture into the hollowed-out squash. After that, sprinkle the last of the parmesan on top, and broil for three more minutes.
- Top with crushed red pepper and chopped basil, then serve immediately.
Nutritional Value: Cal: 223, Protein: 10.2g, Carbohydrates: 23.3g, Fiber: 8.6g, Fat: 10.9g, Sat. Fat: 5.7g

Angel Hair with Asparagus-Kale Pesto

Preparation Time: 10 minutes
Cooking Time: 10 minutes
Servings: 6
Ingredients:

- ¾ pound asparagus, woody ends removed, and coarsely chopped
- ¼ pound kale, thoroughly washed
- ½ cup grated Asiago cheese
- ¼ cup fresh basil
- ¼ cup extra-virgin olive oil
- Juice of 1 lemon
- Sea salt

- Freshly ground black pepper
- 1-pound angel hair pasta
- Zest of 1 lemon

Direction

- Place the kale and asparagus in a food processor and pulse until the vegetables are very finely chopped.
- To create a smooth pesto, add the Asiago cheese, basil, olive oil, and lemon juice, and pulse all of the ingredients together.
- Season with freshly ground black pepper and sea salt, and leave aside.
- Cook the pasta until it is firm to the bite in accordance with the instructions on the box. After draining, transfer the contents to a big basin.
- Add the pesto and mix it very thoroughly so that it coats everything.
- Finish by sprinkling lemon zest over the dish, then serve.
- The asparagus pesto may be made up to three days in advance and stored in the refrigerator. Maintain it in the refrigerator till it is required.

Nutritional Value: Calories: 283; Total Fat: 12g; Saturated Fat: 2g; Carbohydrates: 33g; Fiber: 2g; Protein: 10g

Spicy Pasta Puttanesca

Preparation Time: 10 minutes
Cooking Time: 20 minutes
Servings: 4

Ingredients:

- 2 teaspoons extra-virgin olive oil
- ½ sweet onion, finely chopped
- 2 teaspoons minced garlic
- 1 (28-ounce) can sodium-free diced tomatoes
- ½ cup chopped anchovies
- 2 teaspoons chopped fresh oregano
- 2 teaspoons chopped fresh basil
- ½ teaspoon red pepper flakes
- ½ cup quartered Kalamata olives
- ¼ cup sodium-free chicken broth
- 1 tablespoon capers, drained and rinsed
- Juice of 1 lemon
- 4 cups cooked whole-grain penne

Direction

- Bring the olive oil to a simmer in a large saucepan set over a medium heat.
- After the onion and garlic have been sautéed for about three minutes, the onion should be tender.
- Add the tomatoes, anchovies, oregano, basil, and red pepper flakes to the pot, and stir to combine. Bring the sauce up to a boil, then immediately turn the heat down to a low setting. Maintain a simmer for fifteen minutes while stirring the mixture regularly.
- Add the olives, chicken stock, capers, and lemon juice to a mixing bowl and stir to combine.
- Cook the pasta in accordance with the instructions provided on the package, and then serve it topped with the sauce.
- A word of caution regarding an ingredient: despite the fact that both sardines and anchovies are available in cans and have a silvery appearance, sardines should not be confused with anchovies. In most cases, anchovies are aged in brine before being salted, which produces a flavor that is unique and full-bodied.

  Nutritional Value: Calories: 303; Total Fat: 6g; Saturated Fat: 0g; Carbohydrates: 54g; Fiber: 9g; Protein: 9g

PIZZA RECIPES

Shrimp Pizza

Preparation Time: 15 minutes

Cooking Time: 10 minutes

Serving: 1

Ingredients:

- 2 tablespoons spaghetti sauce
- 1 tablespoon pesto sauce
- 1 (6-inch) pita bread
- 2 tablespoons mozzarella cheese, shredded
- 5 cherry tomatoes, halved
- 1/8 cup bay shrimp
- Pinch of garlic powder
- Pinch of dried basil

Direction

- Put the oven on to preheat at 325 degrees Fahrenheit. Prepare a baking sheet by greasing it very lightly.
- Combine the pesto and spaghetti sauce in a bowl and stir until combined.
- Apply a thin coating of the pesto mixture to the pita bread and spread it out evenly.
- Spread some cheese over the pita bread, then top it with some tomato slices and shrimp.
- Top with a mixture of garlic powder and chopped basil.
- Arrange the pita bread in a single layer on the baking sheet that has been prepared, and bake for approximately 7-10 minutes.
- When ready to cut, remove from the oven and let stand for approximately three to five minutes.
- Slice the meat into the proper thickness, and serve.

    Nutritional Value: Calories 482 Total Fat 18.9 g Saturated Fat 7.8 g Cholesterol 119 mg Total Carbs 44.5 g Sugar 6.6 g Fiber 3.3 g Sodium 900 mg Potassium 420 mg Protein 33.4 g

Veggie Pizza

Preparation Time: 20 minutes

Cooking Time: 12 minutes

Servings: 6

Ingredients:

- 1 (12-inch) prepared pizza crust

- ¼ teaspoon Italian seasoning
- ¼ teaspoon red pepper flakes, crushed
- 1 cup goat cheese, crumbled
- 1 (14-ounce) can quartered artichoke hearts
- 3 plum tomatoes, sliced into ¼-inch thick size
- 6 kalamata olives, pitted and sliced
- ¼ cup fresh basil, chopped

  Direction
- Bring the temperature of the oven up to 450 degrees Fahrenheit. Prepare a baking sheet by greasing it.
- Evenly distribute Italian seasoning and crushed red pepper flakes over the surface of the pizza crust.
- Spread the goat cheese out evenly over the pie crust, leaving approximately a half an inch of crust around the edges.
- Using the back of a spoon, push the cheese in a downward motion until it is flat.
- Atop the cheese, arrange the artichoke hearts, tomatoes, and olives in a single layer.
- Arrange the pizza dough in a single layer on the baking sheet that has been prepared.
- Place in oven and cook for approximately 10 to 12 minutes, or until cheese gets bubbling.
- Take out of the oven and sprinkle with basil before serving.
- Cut the pizza into slices of uniform size, and serve.

  Nutritional Value: Calories 381 Total Fat 16.1 g Saturated Fat 9.8 g Cholesterol 40 mg Total Carbs 42.4 g Sugar 8 g Fiber 5.4 g Sodium 710 mg Potassium 393 mg Protein 19.4 g

Watermelon Feta & Balsamic Pizza

Preparation time: 5 minutes
Cooking Time: 15 minutes
Serving: 4

Ingredients:
- Watermelon (1-inch thick from the center)
- Crumbled feta cheese (1 oz.)
- Sliced Kalamata olives (5-6)
- Mint leaves (1 tsp.)
- Balsamic glaze (.5 tbsp.)

Direction
- Locate the piece of the watermelon that is the widest and cut it in half. After that, cut each half into four equal-sized wedges.

- Place on a pizza round in a circular pie dish and top with the olives, cheese, mint leaves, and glaze.
  Nutritional Value: Protein: 2 grams Fat: 3 grams Calories: 90

White Pizza with Prosciutto and Arugula

Preparation Time: 10 minutes
Cooking Time: 15 minutes
Servings: 6
Ingredients:

- 1 pound prepared pizza dough
- ½ cup ricotta cheese
- 1 tablespoon garlic, minced
- 1 cup grated mozzarella cheese
- 3 ounces prosciutto, thinly sliced
- ½ cup fresh arugula
- ½ teaspoon freshly ground black pepper

Direction

- Bring the oven up to 450 degrees Fahrenheit. On a surface that has been dusted with flour, roll out the pizza dough.
- Place the pizza dough on a baking sheet or pizza sheet that has been coated with parchment paper. Bake the dough for a total of 8 minutes once it has been placed in the oven.
- In a low-sided bowl, combine the ricotta, the garlic, and the mozzarella cheese.
- Take the pizza dough out of the oven and sprinkle it with the cheese mixture after it has cooled somewhat. Continue baking for an additional 5 to 6 minutes.
- Place some pepper, arugula, and prosciutto on top of the pizza, and then serve it warm.
  Nutritional Value: Calories: 73; Protein: 12.3g; Carbs: 3.4g; Fat: 6.3g

Za'atar Pizza

Preparation Time: 10 minutes
Cooking Time: 15 minutes
Servings: 5
Ingredients:

- 1 sheet puff pastry
- ¼ cup extra-virgin olive oil
- 1/3 cup za'atar seasoning

Direction

- Pre-heat the oven to 350 degrees Fahrenheit.
- Place the puff pastry on a baking sheet that has been lined with parchment paper. Prepare the pastry by slicing it into the required shapes.
- Brush the olive oil on top of the pastry. The za'atar should be sprinkled on top.
- Place the pie in the oven and bake for ten to twelve minutes, or until the edges are golden brown and the pastry has risen up. Prepare and serve either hot or at room temperature.
  Nutritional Value: Calories: 53; Protein: 10.3g; Carbs: 3.4g; Fat: 6.3g

Pizza Dough On Yogurt

Preparation Time: 10 minutes
Cooking Time: 30 minutes
Servings: 5
Ingredients:
- Natural yogurt 250 g
- Vegetable oil 5 tablespoons
- ½ teaspoon salt
- Wheat flour 2.5 cups
- Baking powder 1 teaspoon
  Direction
- Combine the flour, baking powder, and salt in a mixing bowl.
- Combine everything completely before adding the butter and yogurt;
- Set the oven's temperature to 190 degrees Celsius;
- Add some oil to the pan to grease it;
- Roll the dough out to an extremely thin thickness and place it on a baking sheet;
- Season the filling to your liking;
- Bake for 10-15 minutes.
  Nutritional Value: Calories: 336; Protein: 10.3g; Carbs: 3.4g; Fat: 13.3g

American Pizza Dough Recipe

Preparation Time: 10 minutes
Cooking Time: 15 minutes
Servings: 5
Ingredients:
- Wheat flour 170 g
- Chicken egg 1 piece
- Water 85 ml
- Dry yeast 2 g

- Salt 3 g
- Sugar 10 g
- Sunflower oil 5 ml
  Direction
- Mix all of the dry ingredients together.
- Add water and egg. Combine thoroughly.
- When the dough has reached a uniform consistency, begin incorporating the butter in a slow and steady manner.
- Give the dough a further five minutes to rest.
  Nutritional Value: Calories: 353; Protein: 10.3g; Carbs: 3.4g; Fat: 13.3g

Sprouts Pizza

Preparation time: 25 minutes
Cooking Time: 15 minutes
Serving: 6
Ingredients:
- 4 oz wheat flour, whole grain
- 2 tablespoons olive oil
- ¼ teaspoon baking powder
- 5 oz chicken fillet, boiled
- 2 oz Mozzarella cheese, shredded
- 1 tomato, chopped
- 2 oz bean sprouts
  Direction
- First, prepare the pizza crust by combining the wheat flour, olive oil, and baking powder into a dough and kneading it.
- Form it into the shape of a pizza crust by rolling it up, and then place it in the pizza mold.
- After that, top it with a mixture of shredded chicken, diced tomato, and mozzarella cheese.
- Bake the pizza for 15 minutes at 365 degrees Fahrenheit.
- After the pizza has finished cooking, sprinkle it with bean sprouts and cut it into individual portions.
  Nutritional Value: 184 calories,11.9g protein, 15.6g carbohydrates, 8.2g fat, 0.6g fiber, 26mg cholesterol, 79mg sodium, 141mg potassium.

Cheese Pinwheels

Preparation time: 20 minutes
Cooking Time: 25 minutes
Serving: 4

Ingredients:

- 1 teaspoon chili flakes
- ½ teaspoon dried cilantro
- 1 egg, beaten
- 1 teaspoon cream cheese
- 1 oz Cheddar cheese, grated
- 6 oz pizza dough

Direction

- Roll the pizza dough into a log and then cut it into six equal squares.
- After the dough has risen, sprinkle it with dried cilantro, cream cheese, and Cheddar cheese.
- Roll the dough into pinwheel shapes, brush with egg that has been beaten, and bake in an oven that has been prepared to 365 degrees Fahrenheit for 25 minutes, or until the pinwheels are golden brown.

Nutritional Value: 16 calories, 3.8g protein, 12.1g carbohydrates, 11.2g fat, 1g fiber, 33mg cholesterol, 178mg sodium, 33mg potassium.

Ground Meat Pizza

Preparation time: 15 minutes
Cooking Time: 35 minutes
Serving: 4

Ingredients:

- 7 oz ground beef
- 1 teaspoon tomato paste
- ½ teaspoon ground black pepper
- 2 egg whites, whisked
- ½ cup Mozzarella cheese, shredded
- 1 teaspoon fresh basil, chopped

Direction

- Place a piece of baking paper on the baking sheet. Prepare the oven to 370 degrees Fahrenheit.
- In a mixing bowl, combine all of the ingredients other than the mozzarella.

- Next, spread the ingredients out evenly in the baking dish using a spatula to form a thick layer.
- Sprinkle mozzarella cheese over the pizza, then place it in the oven to bake for thirty-five minutes.
- After the pizza has finished cooking, cut it into individual portions.
  Nutritional Value: 113 calories, 18g protein, 0.7g carbohydrates, 3.8g fat, 0.1g fiber, 46mg cholesterol, 72mg sodium, 244mg potassium.

MEAT: PORK, LAMB & BEEF RECIPES

Mediterranean Pork Kabobs

Preparation time: 15 minutes
Cooking time: 30 minutes
Serving: 4

Ingredients:

- 1-pound boneless pork loin (or 4 boneless pork chops)
- 6 ounces marinated artichoke hearts
- 1 red bell pepper (seeded and cut into 1-inch squares)
- 1 teaspoon hot pepper sauce
- 1 teaspoon oregano
- 2 tablespoons lemon juice
- 2 teaspoons black pepper

Direction

- Cut the pork loin or chops into pieces that are an inch long, then place them in a bag that can close itself. After draining the artichoke hearts, remove the artichoke hearts and bell pepper squares from the marinade and put them aside. Reserve the marinade for later use.
- Place the additional ingredients in the bag, then add the remaining marinade. Give everything a good mix, and then seal the bag.
- Allow the bag to stand for thirty minutes while turning it periodically (or refrigerate overnight). Prepare medium-hot coals on a grill that has a cover. Skewer the pork, artichoke hearts, and pepper squares. Cook for 15 minutes, or until the meat is cooked through and has a nice browning.
Nutritional Value: Calories: 446 kcal | Protein 76 grams | Carbs: 55 grams | Fat: 25 grams

Mediterranean Meatball and Orzo Bowls

Preparation time: 15 minutes
Cooking time: 30 minutes
Serving: 4

Ingredients:

- 1-pound ground turkey thigh (not turkey breast)
- 1/2 cup panko breadcrumbs
- 1 large egg
- 3 garlic cloves (minced)

- lemon zest (from 1 lemon, about 1 teaspoon; save juice for orzo)
- 1 tablespoon chopped fresh dill (for meatballs)
- 1 teaspoon dried oregano
- 1/2 teaspoon ground cumin
- 1/4 teaspoon salt (plus more to taste)
- 1/4 teaspoon black pepper
- 2 tablespoons extra-virgin olive oil (for meatballs)
- 12 ounces orzo pasta (12 ounces is 1 1/2 cups)
- 1 tablespoon extra-virgin olive oil (for orzo)
- 1 tablespoon lemon juice
- 2 tablespoons fresh dill (leaves)
- 1-pint grape tomatoes (halved)
- 1 English cucumber (cut into chunks)
- 1 1/2 cups pitted kalamata olives (halved)
- 1 small red onion (thinly sliced)
- 12 ounces tzatziki sauce (store-bought)

Direction

- In a medium mixing basin, combine the ground turkey, panko, egg, garlic, lemon zest, dill for meatballs, oregano, cumin, salt, and pepper. This will be the meatball mixture. Create 12 meatballs of equal size using the ingredients; each one should be equivalent to 2 tablespoons.
- Bring a large saucepan of water to a boil before proceeding.
- Place the olive oil that will be used for the meatballs in a big skillet and heat it over medium-high heat until it is hot. Cook the meatballs in a skillet over medium heat, turning them occasionally, for about ten minutes, or until they are browned on both sides and cooked all the way through (cut to check). Take the dish out of the oven and keep it warm.
- While the meatballs are browning, prepare the orzo by cooking it in boiling water until it reaches the desired texture, following the recommendations on the box. After the orzo has been drained, transfer it to a bowl and stir in the olive oil. Remove some orzo and place it on each of the children's plates. To ensure that the leftover orzo is evenly coated, toss it with the lemon juice and dill. Salt and pepper can be added to taste as a seasoning.
- Arrange the orzo in its most basic form, some meatballs, and the children's chosen vegetables (tomatoes, cucumbers, olives, and red onion) on each of their plates. Tzatziki sauce should be served on the side as an accompaniment.
- Distribute the seasoned orzo in an equal amount into each of the serving bowls for the adults' plates. Tzatziki served on a layer of meatballs. Before plating, combine the meatballs and orzo by tossing them with the tomatoes, cucumbers, olives, and onion.

Nutritional Value: Calories: 754 kcal | Protein 49 grams | Carbs: 75 grams | Fat: 15 grams

Mediterranean Pork Chops

Preparation time: 15 minutes
Cooking time: 15 minutes
Serving: 4
Ingredients:

- 2 tablespoons olive oil
- 4 bone-in pork chops (or boneless pork chops)
- 1 red bell pepper (large, or green bell pepper, sliced)
- 1 jar Ragu® Chunky Pasta Sauce (1 lb. 8 oz.)

Direction

- In a skillet of 12 inches in diameter and containing 1 tablespoon of olive oil, sear pork chops on all sides over medium-high heat. Remove from skillet.
- In the same skillet, heat the one tablespoon of olive oil that is left, and sauté the green pepper over medium heat until it is tender.
- Add the Pasta Sauce and thoroughly combine the ingredients. Bring to a boil over a high heat setting. After bringing the temperature down to a low setting, put the pork chops back into the skillet.
- Continue to simmer the beef with the lid on for another ten minutes, or until it is fully done.

Nutritional Value: Calories: 366 kcal | Protein 27 grams | Carbs: 42 grams | Fat: 65 grams

Mediterranean Grilled Steak

Preparation time: 20 minutes
Cooking time: 0 minutes
Refrigerate time: 30 minutes
Serving: 6
Ingredients:

- ½ cup wish-bone (Italian or robusto italian dressing)
- 2 cloves garlic (finely chopped)
- 2 teaspoons sprigs fresh rosemary, torn into pieces
- 1½ pounds steak

Direction

- To make the marinade, combine garlic, rosemary, and Wish-Bone® Italian Dressing in equal parts. Pour a quarter of a cup of the marinade over the steak and turn it to coat it. You may do this in a big, shallow baking dish or in a plastic bag.
- Place in the refrigerator and chill for at least half an hour after covering or securing the bag. Marinate that is left over should be stored in the refrigerator.
- Take the meat out of the marinade and throw away both the meat and the marinade. While grilling the steak to the appropriate degree of doneness, make sure to turn it constantly and often spritz it with the cold marinade.
Nutritional Value: Calories: 543 kcal | Protein 37 grams | Carbs: 52 grams | Fat: 55 grams

Barbecue Bacon-Wrapped Shrimp with Basil Stuffing

Preparation time: 15 minutes

Cooking time: 25 minutes

Serving: 6

Ingredients:

- 32 shrimp (fresh or frozen, in shells)
- 16 slices bacon (cut in half)
- 32 leaves basil (coarsely chopped)
- 2 teaspoons Parmesan cheese (freshly grated)
- 2 cloves garlic (minced)
- 1 cup barbecue sauce

Direction

- If the shrimp are frozen, you will need to thaw them before continuing. You should take the shrimp's shells off, but you should save the tails. Remove the vein from each shrimp by cutting a slit down the rear of it and removing it. Shrimp may be made clean by giving them a quick rinse in water and then drying them off with paper towels.
- For the filling, combine chopped basil, grated Parmesan cheese, and minced garlic in a separate dish. Fill the slits that have been made in the meat. Wrap each shrimp with a half slice of bacon, ensuring that the ends are tucked in, but exposing the tail.
- Set the temperature in the oven to four hundred degrees Fahrenheit. The shrimp should have their tails facing upward when they are placed on the baking sheet. Bake the shrimp for approximately 14 minutes, or until they become opaque. Use paper towels to soak up any surplus liquid that may have been spilled.
- Place back on baking sheet and continue roasting for approximately 3 minutes, or until the sauce has browned. Dip shrimp in barbecue sauce and set on grill until sauce caramelizes.

Nutritional Value: Calories: 653 kcal | Protein 43 grams | Carbs: 67 grams | Fat: 30 grams

Lebanese Meat Pies

Preparation time: 1 hours

Cooking time: 35 minutes

Servings: 24

Ingredients:

- 1 package of dough or 1 package of Rhodes 36 count frozen dinner rolls
- 1 to 1½ pounds of ground beef or lamb {I used 80/20}
- 1 sweet onion, finely chopped
- 4 garlic cloves, minced
- 1 teaspoon cumin
- 2 Tablespoons olive oil
- 1 teaspoon cinnamon
- ½ teaspoon allspice
- ¼ teaspoon cloves
- ¼ teaspoon cayenne pepper {optional}
- ¼ teaspoon salt
- 1/8 teaspoon black pepper

Direction

- Before using the frozen dough, defrost it in the refrigerator for six to twelve hours. After being defrosted, the dough will not rise, but it will be suitable for use at that point.
- Using a spray that prevents sticking, coat two baking pans. Spread the dough out on the baking sheet and cover it with a kitchen towel to allow it to rise for about an hour if you are not using frozen rolls. After the dough has doubled in size, roll it into balls approximately 2 inches in diameter and make around 24 in total. Allow the dough to continue to rise for another half an hour while it is covered with a dish towel.
- If you are using frozen roll dough, divide it evenly between two baking pans and place 24 frozen dough rolls on each pan. Following the application of nonstick spray, cover the dough with plastic wrap and set it aside. Please allow the dough to thaw and rise for about two to three hours.
- Set the temperature in the oven to four hundred degrees Fahrenheit.
- To begin preparing the beef combo, begin by dicing the steak into small pieces. 2 tablespoons of olive oil, warmed in a skillet of medium size over a medium heat. Sauté the garlic and onion for two to three minutes, or until they reach the desired level of tenderness. While the ground beef or lamb is being cooked, the spices should be cooked

alongside it until the meat is browned. After removing the excess fat from the ground beef, transfer it to a mixing bowl.

- Before beginning to create the meat pies, you will need to prepare a large cutting board or another type of work surface that has lots of area for rolling out the dough. Dust the area that you'll be working on with flour. With the use of a rolling pin, flatten each ball of dough until it has three sides.
- Fill each dough circle just halfway with the beef mixture, leaving room around the edges to use as a seal when you bake the pies.
- Form a point in the middle of the dough by bringing the three sides of the dough together. Make sure the dough is completely sealed by pinching it together with your fingers once it has been brought together.
- Coat each meat pie with a little olive oil by brushing it on with an olive oil brush or spraying it with olive oil.
- Preheat the oven to 350 degrees Fahrenheit and bake the chicken for twenty minutes, or until the top is golden brown. In the final two minutes of baking, raise the temperature to 450 degrees to get a beautiful golden brown on the edges of the baked good.
- Take the dish out of the oven and allow it to cool for a few minutes before serving.
- Prepare immediately or put in the freezer for use at a later time.
Nutritional Value: Calories: 446 kcal | Protein 76 grams | Carbs: 55 grams | Fat: 25 grams

Easy Mediterranean Burers

Preparation time: 20 minutes
Cooking time: 10 minutes
Servings: 4
Ingredients:
- 2 pounds Certified Angus Beef ® ground chuck
- 1/4 cup roasted red peppers, finely chopped
- 2 tablespoons chopped fresh parsley
- 1/2 teaspoon oregano
- 1 teaspoon cumin
- 1/2 teaspoon paprika
- 1/8 teaspoon garlic powder
- 1 teaspoon salt
- 1/8 teaspoon black pepper
 For Servings:
- 4 Hamburger buns
- Crumbled feta cheese

- Roasted red peppers, chopped
- Fresh arugula

Direction

- Mix together the ground chuck, roasted red peppers, parsley, oregano, cumin, paprika, garlic powder, salt, and pepper in a large mixing bowl.
- Cook to an internal temperature of 160° F by dividing the mixture into four patties.
- Burgers should be served on buns with crumbled feta cheese, roasted red peppers, and fresh arugula on top.

Nutritional Value: Calories: 754 kcal | Protein 49 grams | Carbs: 75 grams | Fat: 15 grams

Greek Beef Pita Pizza

Preparation time: 20 minutes

Cooking time: 15 minutes

Servings: 4

Ingredients:

- 2 Tablespoons ghee {clarified butter}, butter or olive oil
- 1-pound Certified Angus Beef ® brand ground beef
- 1/4 teaspoon salt
- Dash of pepper
- 1 teaspoon oregano
- 1/2 teaspoon basil
- 1/4 teaspoon cayenne pepper {optional}
- 4 - 6-inch pita bread rounds {try whole wheat for a healthier version}
- 1 cup of your favorite hummus, divided
- 1/4 cup red onion, diced
- 1 cup diced fresh tomatoes, divided
- 1 cup cucumber, diced
- 1/2 cup feta cheese, crumbled
- 1 cup kalamata olives, pitted and sliced in half
- 1/2 cup fresh parsley, chopped, divided
- 1/2 cup pepperoncinis, sliced {optional}

Direction

- Preheat oven to 350 degrees Fahrenheit.
- Two tablespoons of ghee, butter, or olive oil, melted in a large saucepan over medium heat The ground beef should be seasoned with salt and pepper before being cooked in a skillet until it is browned. The oregano, basil, and cayenne pepper should be set aside once the excess fat has been drained.

49

- Arrange your four pita rounds in a single layer on a baking sheet, and then bake them for twenty minutes. A very thin layer of hummus should be put on each of them. On top of the dish, serve ground beef that has been cooked.
- Set the oven temperature to 350 degrees Fahrenheit and bake the pita for 5-7 minutes, or until it starts to get crisp. On top of the salad, sprinkle some red onion, tomato, cucumber, feta cheese, olives, parsley, and pepperoncini.
  Nutritional Value: Calories: 876kcal | Protein 43 grams | Carbs: 51 grams | Fat: 32 grams

Mediterranean Pork Chop

Preparation time: 15 minutes

Cooking time; 15 minutes

Servings: 4

Ingredients:

- 1-pint grape tomatoes (halved)
- 1 teaspoon olive oil
- 1/4 teaspoon kosher salt
- 1 teaspoon dried thyme
- cooking spray
- 8 center cut boneless pork chops (thin sliced, 1/2-inch)
- 1 tablespoon Greek seasoning blend
- 12 ounces zucchini spirals (and yellow squash veggie spirals)
- 1 pinch salt
- 1 pinch black pepper
- 1/4 cup kalamata olives (pitted and sliced)
- 1/4 cup garbanzo beans (rinsed and drained)
- 1/4 cup crumbled feta
- 1/2 lemon (juiced)
- 1 teaspoon lemon zest
- 1/4 cup chopped parsley

Direction

- Place a baking sheet in the oven and preheat it to 450 degrees Fahrenheit.
- Place the tomatoes and olive oil in a bowl and toss to combine. Add some thyme, salt, and pepper before serving. Prepare the tomatoes by baking them on a baking pan that has been coated with cooking spray. Roast the tomatoes for fifteen to twenty minutes, turning them once, until they become blistered and begin to pop. Wait until it has cooled down before serving.

- The pork chops are seasoned with a variety of Greek spices. Two separate heat ups are performed in a large nonstick skillet over medium-high heat. Cooking spray is applied to half of the pork chops, and they are seared over medium-high heat for 112 to 2 minutes per side until an internal temperature of 145 degrees Fahrenheit is reached. Place on a platter and let it sit for a while.
- During the time that the pork is resting, add the vegetable spirals to the same pan and cook them over medium-high heat. Add little salt and pepper before serving. Sauté the veggies for around two to three minutes, or until they reach the desired level of tenderness. Mix in the garnish, as well as the tomatoes that have been roasted. Mix along with the pork chops, then serve.
  Nutritional Value: Calories: 342 kcal | Protein 33 grams | Carbs: 67 grams | Fat: 12 grams

Hummus With Spiced Beef and Toasted Pine Nuts

Preparation time: 20 minutes

Cooking time: 20 minutes

Servings: 6

Ingredients:

For the hummus:

- 1 -16 oz can of chickpeas (garbanzo beans), drained and rinsed
- Juice of 1 lemon
- 1/3 cup tahini
- 1 or 2 cloves garlic
- 3 tablespoons extra virgin olive oil {you may want more for thinner hummus}
- Parsley and paprika to garnish

For the beef:

- 1 Tablespoon olive oil {or 1 Tablespoon clarified butter ghee}
- 1-pound ground beef, {I use 80/20}
- 1/4 of a sweet onion, chopped
- 2 garlic cloves, minced
- 1 teaspoon cinnamon
- 1 teaspoon allspice
- 1/4 teaspoon cayenne pepper
- 1/4 teaspoon paprika
- 1/4 teaspoon clove

Garnish:

- 1/4 cup pine nuts, toasted
- Freshly chopped tomatoes

- Freshly chopped parsley
- A drizzle of extra virgin olive oil
  Direction

  In order to make hummus:

- Put all of the ingredients into a food processor and process them together. 30 to 60 seconds of mixing time, maximum (blend longer for more creamy texture). In the event that the hummus is excessively thick, dilute it by adding a minuscule amount of extra virgin olive oil and mix it once more.
- Take that variable out of the equation.
- With regard to the beef:
- In a large saucepan, bring the ghee (or olive oil) to a simmer over medium-high heat. After waiting for the onion to become translucent in the pan, add the garlic along with it. Adjust the temperature so that it is medium and then add the ground beef.
- Using a wooden spoon, begin to break up the ground beef and start the cooking process. Cook the ground beef together with the cinnamon, allspice, cayenne pepper, paprika, and clove in a skillet until the beef is completely cooked through and no pink color remains.
- Before taking the ground beef off the heat, drain any excess fat that may have accumulated in the pan.
- To prepare the pine nuts that have been toasted:
- Toast the pine nuts in a large, dry pan over medium-low heat, tossing them frequently, until they begin to turn brown in spots. This should take about three minutes. Take the thing out of the way and put it away.
- In a large mixing bowl, combine all of the ingredients for the Hummus Beef with Toasted Pine Nuts recipe.
- Arrange your hummus in an appropriate platter for presentation. On top of it, layer the ground beef mixture. To finish, add a drizzle of extra virgin olive oil, pine nuts that have been roasted in the oven, sliced tomatoes, and chopped parsley. Pita bread is a delicious option for a side dish.
  Nutritional Value: Calories: 656 kcal | Protein 56 grams | Carbs: 53 grams | Fat: 21 grams

Spiced Beef and Lamb Kebabs

Preparation Time: 15 minutes
Cooking Time: 10 minutes
Serving: 15
Ingredients:
- 1/2-pound ground beef 15% fat recommended

- 1/2-pound ground lamb
- 1 cup diced yellow onions (about 1 small onion)
- 1/2 cup chickpea/garbanzo bean flour see headnote above
- 1 large egg
- 2 fresh Thai chilis, minced see headnote above
- 2 medium garlic cloves, minced
- 1 inch piece of ginger, peeled and grated
- 1 tablespoon lime juice
- Zest of 1/2 lime
- 1 teaspoon ground coriander
- 1 teaspoon dried mint (about 1/2 bag of mint tea) see headnote above
- 1/2 teaspoon cayenne pepper
- 1/2 teaspoon ground cinnamon
- 1/2 teaspoon ground sage
- 1/2 teaspoon dried dill
- 1/2 teaspoon kosher salt
- 2 tablespoons olive oil
  To garnish:
- 1 tablespoons cilantro leaf
- Thinly sliced red onions

  Direction
- In a large mixing bowl, combine all of the kebab ingredients except the olive oil. To begin, combine all of the ingredients with a wooden spoon until they are uniformly dispersed.
- In a large mixing dish, combine all of the kebab ingredients (except the olive oil).
- Dampen your hands and shape the mixture into 1 1/2-inch wide, 1/2-inch-thick patties. When you're finished, you should have around 14 or 15 patties.
- Form 15 patties from the mixture, each approximately 1 1/2 inches broad and 1/2 inch thick.
- In a large pan, heat the olive oil and cook half of the kebabs for 3 to 4 minutes over medium heat, or until the side of the kebab is a deep golden brown and a crust has developed. Cook until the kebab is cooked through, flipping it over halfway through.
- Fry the kebabs in batches, 3 to 4 minutes each side, until golden brown and crusty.
- Serve the kebabs with thinly sliced red onions and cilantro leaves.
  Nutritional Value: Calories: 964 kcal | Protein 67 grams | Carbs: 55 grams | Fat: 35 grams

Stuffed Baby Eggplant with Spiced Ground Beef, Bulgur and Pine Nuts

Preparation Time: 20 minutes

Cooking Time: 45 minutes

Servings: 4

Ingredients:

- 2 large eggplants, stems removed, halved
- Salt to taste
- Extra virgin olive oil
- 1 medium yellow onion, shredded (about ½ cup packed shredded yellow onion)
- 2 large garlic cloves, chopped
- ¾ lb. lean ground beef (you can use ground turkey or lamb as well)
- 1 tsp ground allspice, divided
- 1 tsp ground cinnamon, divided
- ¼ cup extra-fine bulgur, soaked in ¼ cup hot water for 10 minutes then drained (bulgur must be extra fine)
- ½ cup packed chopped fresh parsley
- ¼ cup toasted pine nuts
- 1 15 oz can tomato sauce
- 1 cup water
- 1 red onion, sliced into rings
- Topping suggestions (optional)

Direction

- Place a baking sheet in the oven and preheat it to 425 degrees Fahrenheit.
- Arrange the eggplant in a single layer on a large tray, flesh side facing up. After seasoning the flesh with salt and setting it aside for twenty minutes, the astringent fluids of the eggplant will have had time to "sweat." To get rid of the acrid fluids, squeeze the eggplant while holding it over the sink. Apply some dryness with a fresh cloth.
- Prepare a baking sheet by first covering it with aluminum foil and then lightly coating it with oil. The flesh of the eggplant should have three slits or shallow lines cut into it, and then it should be generously coated with olive oil. Place the meaty side down on the tray that has been prepared. The top should be finished with a few more drops of extra virgin olive oil.
- Place in a hot oven and roast for thirty minutes, or until the flesh is tender and golden all the way through (but not burned).
- While the eggplant is roasting, prepare the stuffing mixture using the ground beef. 2 tablespoons of extra virgin olive oil, heated in a large, heavy pan. In a large mixing basin, combine the garlic, onions, and ground meat. To ensure that the beef is cooked through, continue to cook it over a heat that is medium-high. The beef mixture should be

seasoned with salt and pepper, as well as 12 teaspoons each of allspice and ground cinnamon.

- Take the pan off the burner and set it aside. Before adding it to the meat mixture, squeeze the bulgur to remove any excess water and then mix it in. Chopped parsley and pine nuts are included. Give the ingredients a thorough stir. If required, adjust the salt to your own preference (do not over-salt, especially if using salted tomato sauce later)
- Take the eggplant out of the oven and let it cool for a few minutes before proceeding with the recipe. Bring the temperature inside the oven down to 375 degrees Fahrenheit.
- In a small bowl, combine the tomato sauce, water, and the rest of the cinnamon and spices.
- Line the bottom of a casserole dish with red onion slices and then fill with 12 tablespoons of the tomato sauce mixture. The dish should be covered completely. Arrange the roasted eggplant on top of the dish.
- Using the back of a spoon, gently push the flesh of the eggplant down to make room for the meat filling mixture. Put the meat stuffing mixture you created in the eggplant cavities you cut out earlier. Complete the dish by adding the leftover combination of tomato sauce.
- Wrap the casserole dish completely in aluminum foil. Bake the dish for 20 to 25 minutes after preheating the oven to 375 degrees Fahrenheit.
- Serve while still warm, accompanying each portion with a side of Zhoug, Greek Tzatziki, or plain yogurt. Make sure you use some warm pita bread or your preferred type of crusty bread to soak up all of the flavor!

Nutritional Value: Calories: 433 kcal | Protein 47 grams | Carbs: 55 grams | Fat: 15 grams

FISH & SEAFOOD RECIPES

Grilled Salmon

Preparation Time: 15 minutes

Cooking Time: 16 minutes

Servings: 6

Ingredients:

- 1½ pounds salmon fillet
- Pepper to taste
- Garlic powder to taste
- 1/3 cup soy sauce
- 1/3 cup of brown sugar
- 1/3 cup of water
- 1/4 cup vegetable oil

Direction

- Sprinkle the lemon pepper, salt, and garlic powder over the salmon fillets before cooking.
- In a small bowl, combine the brown sugar, water, vegetable oil, and soy sauce. Stir the mixture until the sugar is completely dissolved. Marinate the salmon for at least two hours by placing it in a large plastic bag that can be sealed, adding the soy sauce mixture, and then sealing the bag.
- Bring the grill up to a medium temperature before using it.
- Coat the grill with a thin layer of oil. After the grill has been hot, put the salmon on it and throw away the marinade. Salmon should be cooked for 6 to 8 minutes per side, or until it flakes readily when tested with a fork.

Nutritional Value: 318 calories 20.1 grams of fat 13.2 g carbohydrates 20.5 g of protein 56 mg cholesterol 1092 mg of sodium

Dijon Mustard and Lime Marinated Shrimp

Preparation Time: 10 minutes

Cooking Time: 10 minutes

Servings: 8

Ingredients:

- ½ cup fresh lime juice, plus lime zest as garnish
- ½ cup rice vinegar
- ½ teaspoon hot sauce
- 1 bay leaf

- 1 cup water
- 1 lb. uncooked shrimp, peeled and deveined
- 1 medium red onion, chopped
- 2 tablespoon capers
- 2 tablespoon Dijon mustard
- 3 whole cloves

Direction

- In a pie plate or other shallow baking dish, combine hot sauce, mustard, capers, lime juice, and onion, then put aside.
- In a large saucepan, bring the cloves, bay leaf, and water to a boil, then add the vinegar.
- Once the liquid has reached a boil, add the shrimp and continue to stir while cooking for one minute.
- After the shrimp have been drained, add them to the combination of onions.
- Place the shrimp in the refrigerator and keep them covered for the next hour.
- After that, serve the shrimp chilled and garnish them with the zest of one lime.

Nutritional Value: Calories: 232.2; Protein: 17.8g; Fat: 3g; Carbs: 15g

Dill Relish on White Sea Bass

Preparation Time: 10 minutes

Cooking Time: 12 minutes

Servings: 4

Ingredients:

- 1 ½ tablespoon chopped white onion
- 1 ½ teaspoon chopped fresh dill
- 1 lemon, quartered
- 1 teaspoon Dijon mustard
- 1 teaspoon lemon juice
- 1 teaspoon pickled baby capers, drained
- 4 pieces of 4-oz white sea bass fillets

Direction

- Preheat oven to 375 degrees Fahrenheit.
- In a small bowl, combine the lemon juice, mustard, dill, capers, and chopped onions.
- Prepare four aluminum foil squares and insert 1 fillet each foil.
- Squeeze half of a lemon slice over each piece of fish.
- Distribute the dill spread in four equal parts and pour it over the fillet.
- Ensure that the foil is well closed over the fish, and then place it in the oven.
- Place the fish in the oven and cook for ten to twelve minutes, or until it is fully done.

- After removing the food from the foil, put it to a serving tray, and then serve and enjoy the meal.
Nutritional Value: Calories: 115; Protein: 7g; Fat: 1g; Carbs: 12g

Sweet Potatoes Oven Fried

Preparation time: 10 minutes
Cooking time: 30 minutes
Servings: 7
Ingredients:

- 1 small garlic clove, minced
- 1 teaspoon grated orange rind
- 1 tablespoon fresh parsley, chopped finely
- ¼ teaspoon pepper
- ¼ teaspoon salt
- 1 tablespoon olive oil
- 4 medium sweet potatoes, peeled and sliced to ¼-inch thickness
Direction
- Place the sweet potatoes, pepper, salt, and olive oil in a large basin and stir until thoroughly combined.
- On a baking sheet that has been oiled, place the sweet potatoes in a single layer.
- Place in an oven that has been prepared to 400 degrees Fahrenheit and bake for 15 minutes. After baking, flip the potato slices over and return to the oven. Continue baking for another 15 minutes, or until the vegetables are soft.
- In the meantime, thoroughly combine the garlic, orange rind, and parsley in a small dish. Then, sprinkle the mixture over the potato slices that have been cooked and serve.
- If you bake sweet potatoes and store them in a jar with a lid, you can reheat them in the microwave anytime you want to eat them. Consume throughout a period of three days.
Nutritional Value: Calories: 176; Carbs: 36.6g; Protein: 2.5g; Fat: 2.5g

Tasty Avocado Sauce over Zoodles

Preparation time: 10 minutes
Cooking time: 10 minutes
Servings: 2
Ingredients:

- 1 zucchini peeled and spiralized into noodles
- 4 tablespoon pine nuts
- 2 tablespoon lemon juice

- 1 avocado peeled and pitted
- 12 sliced cherry tomatoes
- 1/3 cup water
- 1 1/4 cup basil
- Pepper and salt to taste

Directions:

- Make the sauce in a blender by adding pine nuts, lemon juice, avocado, water, and basil. Pulse until smooth and creamy. Season with pepper and salt to taste. Mix well.
- Place zoodles in salad bowl. Pour over avocado sauce and toss well to coat.
- Add cherry tomatoes, serve, and enjoy.

Nutritional Value: Calories: 313; Protein: 6.8g; Carbs: 18.7g; Fat: 26.8g

Tomato Basil Cauliflower Rice

Preparation time: 5 minutes

Cooking time: 10 minutes

Servings: 4

Ingredients:

- Salt and pepper to taste
- Dried parsley for garnish
- ¼ cup tomato paste
- ½ teaspoon garlic, minced
- ½ teaspoon onion powder
- ½ teaspoon marjoram
- 1 ½ teaspoon dried basil
- 1 teaspoon dried oregano
- 1 large head of cauliflower
- 1 teaspoon oil

Directions:

- Cut the cauliflower into florets and place in the food processor.
- Pulse until it has a coarse consistency similar with rice. Set aside.
- In a skillet, heat the oil and sauté the garlic and onion for three minutes. Add the rest of the ingredients. Cook for 8 minutes.

Nutritional Value: Calories: 106; Carbs: 15.1g; Protein: 3.3g; Fat: 5.0g

Vegan Sesame Tofu and Eggplants

Preparation time: 10 minutes

Cooking time: 20 minutes

Servings: 4

Ingredients:

- 5 tablespoons olive oil
- 1-pound firm tofu, sliced
- 3 tablespoons rice vinegar
- 2 teaspoons Swerve sweetener
- 2 whole eggplants, sliced
- ¼ cup soy sauce
- Salt and pepper to taste
- 4 tablespoons toasted sesame oil
- ¼ cup sesame seeds
- 1 cup fresh cilantro, chopped
  Directions:
- Heat the oil in a pan for 2 minutes.
- Pan fry the tofu for 3 minutes on each side.
- Stir in the rice vinegar, sweetener, eggplants, and soy sauce. Season with salt and pepper to taste.
- Cover and cook for 5 minutes on medium fire. Stir and continue cooking for another 5 minutes.
- Toss in the sesame oil, sesame seeds, and cilantro.
- Serve and enjoy.
  Nutritional Value: Calories: 616; Carbs: 27.4g; Protein: 23.9g; Fat: 49.2g

Baked Sea Bass

Preparation time: 10 minutes
Cooking time: 12 minutes
Servings: 4

Ingredients:

- 4 sea bass fillets, boneless
- Salt and black pepper to the taste
- 2 cups potato chips, crushed
- 1 tablespoon mayonnaise

Direction:

- Season the fish fillets with salt and pepper, brush them with mayonnaise and pass them in the chips.
- Arrange the fillets on a baking sheet lined with parchment paper and bake at
- 400°F for 12 minutes.

- Divide the fish on plates and serve with a side salad.
  Nutritional Value: calories 228; fat 8.6g; fiber 0.6g; carbohydrates 9.3g; protein 25g

Fish and Tomato Sauce

Preparation time: 10 minutes
Cooking time: 30 minutes
Servings: 4
Ingredients:

- 4 cod fillets, boneless
- 2 garlic cloves, minced
- 2 cups cherry tomatoes, halved
- 1 cup chicken stock
- A pinch of salt and black pepper
- ¼ cup basil, chopped
Direction:
- Place the tomatoes, garlic, salt and pepper in a pan, heat over medium heat and cook for 5 minutes.
- Add the fish and the rest of the ingredients, bring to a boil, cover the pan and cook for 25 minutes.
- Divide the mix on plates and serve.
  Nutritional Value: calories 180; fat 1.9g; fiber 1.4g; carbohydrates 5.3g; protein 33.8g

Seafood Paella

Preparation time: 20 minutes
Cooking time: 20 minutes
Serving: 4
Ingredients:

- ¼ cup plus 1 tablespoon extra-virgin olive oil
- 1 large onion, finely chopped
- 2 tomatoes, peeled and chopped
- 1½ tablespoons garlic powder
- 1½ cups medium-grain Spanish paella rice or arborio rice
- 2 carrots, finely diced
- Salt, to taste
- 1 tablespoon sweet paprika
- 8 ounces (227 g) lobster meat or canned crab
- ½ cup frozen peas

- 3 cups chicken stock, plus more if needed
- 1 cup dry white wine
- 6 jumbo shrimp, unpeeled
- 1/3-pound (136 g) calamari rings
- 1 lemon, halved

Direction:

- In a large sauté pan or skillet (16-inch is ideal), heat the oil over medium heat until small bubbles start to escape from oil. Add the onion and cook for about 3 minutes, until fragrant, then add tomatoes and garlic powder. Cook for 5 to 10 minutes, until the tomatoes are reduced by half and the consistency is sticky.
- Stir in the rice, carrots, salt, paprika, lobster, and peas and mix well. In a pot or microwave-safe bowl, heat the chicken stock to almost boiling, then add it to the rice mixture. Bring to a simmer, then add the wine.
- Smooth out the rice in the bottom of the pan. Cover and cook on low for 10 minutes, mixing occasionally, to prevent burning.
- Top the rice with the shrimp, cover, and cook for 5 more minutes. Add additional broth to the pan if the rice looks dried out.
- Right before removing the skillet from the heat, add the calamari rings. Toss the Shopping List frequently. In about 2 minutes, the rings will look opaque. Remove the pan from the heat immediately (if you don't want the paella to overcook). Squeeze fresh lemon juice over the dish.

  Nutritional Value: calories: 632 | fat: 20g | protein: 34g | carbohydrates: 71g | fiber: 5g | sodium: 920mg

Escabeche

Preparation time: 10 minutes
Cooking time: 20 minutes
Serving: 4

Ingredients:

- 1 pound (454 g) wild-caught Spanish mackerel fillets, cut into four pieces
- 1 teaspoon salt
- ½ teaspoon freshly ground black pepper
- 8 tablespoons extra-virgin olive oil, divided
- 1 bunch asparagus, trimmed and cut into 2-inch pieces
- 1 (13¾-ounce / 390-g) can artichoke hearts, drained and quartered
- 4 large garlic cloves, peeled and crushed
- 2 bay leaves
- ¼ cup red wine vinegar

- ½ teaspoon smoked paprika

Direction:

- Sprinkle the fillets with salt and pepper and let sit at room temperature for 5 minutes.
- In a large skillet, heat 2 tablespoons olive oil over medium-high heat. Add the fish, skin-side up, and cook 5 minutes. Flip and cook 5 minutes on the other side, until browned and cooked through. Transfer to a serving dish, pour the cooking oil over the fish, and cover to keep warm.
- Heat the remaining 6 tablespoons olive oil in the same skillet over medium heat. Add the asparagus, artichokes, garlic, and bay leaves and sauté until the vegetables are tender, 6 to 8 minutes.
- Using a slotted spoon, top the fish with the cooked vegetables, reserving the oil in the skillet. Add the vinegar and paprika to the oil and whisk to combine well. Pour the vinaigrette over the fish and vegetables and let sit at room temperature for at least 15 minutes, or marinate in the refrigerator up to 24 hours for a deeper flavor. Remove the bay leaf before serving.

  Nutritional Value: calories: 578 | fat: 50g | protein: 26g | carbohydrates: 13g | fiber: 5g | sodium: 946mg

Crispy Sardines

Preparation time: 5 minutes
Cooking time: 5 minutes
Serving: 4

Ingredients:

- Avocado oil, as needed
- 1½ pounds (680 g) whole fresh sardines, scales removed
- 1 teaspoon salt
- 1 teaspoon freshly ground black pepper
- 2 cups flour

Direction

- Preheat a deep skillet over medium heat. Pour in enough oil so there is about 1 inch of it in the pan.
- Season the fish with the salt and pepper.
- Dredge the fish in the flour so it is completely covered.
- Slowly drop in 1 fish at a time, making sure not to overcrowd the pan.
- Cook for about 3 minutes on each side or just until the fish begins to brown on all sides. Serve warm.

Nutritional Value: calories: 794 | fat: 47g | protein: 48g | carbohydrates: 44g | fiber: 2g | sodium: 1441mg

Roasted Salmon

Preparation time: 10 minutes
Cooking time: 25 minutes
Serving: 4

Ingredients:

- ½ cup extra-virgin olive oil, divided
- 2 tablespoons balsamic vinegar
- 2 tablespoons garlic powder, divided
- 1 tablespoon cumin seeds
- 1 teaspoon sea salt, divided
- 1 teaspoon freshly ground black pepper, divided
- 2 teaspoons smoked paprika
- 4 (8-ounce / 227-g) salmon fillets, skinless
- 2 small red onion, thinly sliced
- ½ cup halved Campari tomatoes
- 1 small fennel bulb, thinly sliced lengthwise
- 1 large carrot, thinly sliced
- 8 medium portobello mushrooms
- 8 medium radishes, sliced 1/8 inch thick
- ½ cup dry white wine
- ½ lime, zested
- Handful cilantro leaves
- ½ cup halved pitted Kalamata olives
- 1 orange, thinly sliced
- 4 roasted sweet potatoes, cut in wedges lengthwise

Direction

- Preheat the oven to 375°F (190°C).
- In a medium bowl, mix 6 tablespoons of olive oil, the balsamic vinegar, 1 tablespoon of garlic powder, the cumin seeds, ¼ teaspoon of sea salt, ¼ teaspoon of pepper, and the paprika. Put the salmon in the bowl and marinate while preparing the vegetables, about 10 minutes.
- Heat an oven-safe sauté pan or skillet on medium-high heat and sear the top of the salmon for about 2 minutes, or until lightly brown. Set aside.

- Add the remaining 2 tablespoons of olive oil to the same skillet. Once it's hot, add the onion, tomatoes, fennel, carrot, mushrooms, radishes, the remaining 1 teaspoon of garlic powder, ¾ teaspoon of salt, and ¾ teaspoon of pepper. Mix well and cook for 5 to 7 minutes, until fragrant. Add wine and mix well.
- Place the salmon on top of the vegetable mixture, browned-side up. Sprinkle the fish with lime zest and cilantro and place the olives around the fish. Put orange slices over the fish and cook for about 7 additional minutes. While this is baking, add the sliced sweet potato wedges on a baking sheet and bake this alongside the skillet.
- Remove from the oven, cover the skillet tightly, and let rest for about 3 minutes.
  Nutritional Value: calories: 841 | fat: 41g | protein: 59g | carbohydrates: 60g | fiber: 15g | sodium: 908mg

Almond-Crusted Swordfish

Preparation time: 25 minutes

Cooking time: 15 minutes

Serving: 4

Ingredients:

- ½ cup almond flour
- ¼ cup crushed Marcona almonds
- ½ to 1 teaspoon salt, divided
- 2 pounds (907 g) Swordfish, preferably 1 inch thick
- 1 large egg, beaten (optional)
- ¼ cup pure apple cider
- ¼ cup extra-virgin olive oil, plus more for frying
- 3 to 4 sprigs flat-leaf parsley, chopped
- 1 lemon, juiced
- 1 tablespoon Spanish paprika
- 5 medium baby portobello mushrooms, chopped (optional)
- 4 or 5 chopped scallions, both green and white parts
- 3 to 4 garlic cloves, peeled
- ¼ cup chopped pitted Kalamata olives

Direction

- On a dinner plate, spread the flour and crushed Marcona almonds and mix in the salt. Alternately, pour the flour, almonds, and ¼ teaspoon of salt into a large plastic food storage bag. Add the fish and coat it with the flour mixture. If a thicker coat is desired, repeat this step after dipping the fish in the egg (if using).
- In a measuring cup, combine the apple cider, ¼ cup of olive oil, parsley, lemon juice, paprika, and ¼ teaspoon of salt. Mix well and set aside.

- In a large, heavy-bottom sauté pan or skillet, pour the olive oil to a depth of 1/8 inch and heat on medium heat. Once the oil is hot, add the fish and brown for 3 to 5 minutes, then turn the fish over and add the mushrooms (If using), scallions, garlic, and olives. Cook for an additional 3 minutes. Once the other side of the fish is brown, remove the fish from the pan and set aside.
- Pour the cider mixture into the skillet and mix well with the vegetables. Put the fried fish into the skillet on top of the mixture and cook with sauce on medium-low heat for 10 minutes, until the fish flakes easily with a fork. Carefully remove the fish from the pan and plate. Spoon the sauce over the fish. Serve with white rice or home-fried potatoes. **Nutritional Value:** calories: 620 | fat: 37g | protein: 63g | carbohydrates: 10g | fiber: 5g | sodium: 644mg

Lemon Rosemary Branzino

Preparation time: 15 minutes
Cooking time: 30 minutes
Serving: 2
Ingredients:

- 4 tablespoons extra-virgin olive oil, divided
- 2 (8-ounce / 227-g) branzino fillets, preferably at least 1 inch thick
- 1 garlic clove, minced
- 1 bunch scallions, white part only, thinly sliced
- ½ cup sliced pitted Kalamata or other good-quality black olives
- 1 large carrot, cut into ¼-inch rounds
- 10 to 12 small cherry tomatoes, halved
- ½ cup dry white wine
- 2 tablespoons paprika
- 2 teaspoons kosher salt
- ½ tablespoon ground chili pepper, preferably Turkish or Aleppo
- 2 rosemary sprigs or 1 tablespoon dried rosemary
- 1 small lemon, very thinly sliced
Direction
- Warm a large, oven-safe sauté pan or skillet over high heat until hot, about 2 minutes. Carefully add 1 tablespoon of olive oil and heat until it shimmers, 10 to 15 seconds. Brown the branzino fillets for 2 minutes, skin-side up. Carefully flip the fillets skin-side down and cook for another 2 minutes, until browned. Set aside.
- Swirl 2 tablespoons of olive oil around the skillet to coat evenly. Add the garlic, scallions, kalamata olives, carrot, and tomatoes, and let the vegetables sauté for 5 minutes, until

softened. Add the wine, stirring until all Shopping List are well integrated. Carefully place the fish over the sauce.

- Preheat the oven to 450°F (235°C).
- While the oven is heating, brush the fillets with 1 tablespoon of olive oil and season with paprika, salt, and chili pepper. Top each fillet with a rosemary sprig and several slices of lemon. Scatter the olives over fish and around the pan.
- Roast until lemon slices are browned or singed, about 10 minutes.
  Nutritional Value: calories: 725 | fat: 43g | protein: 58g | carbohydrates: 25g | fiber: 10g | sodium: 2954mg

Black Bean Pasta

Preparation time: 10 minutes
Cooking time: 15 minutes
Serving: 4
Ingredients:

- 1 pound (454 g) black bean linguine or spaghetti
- 1 pound (454 g) fresh shrimp, peeled and deveined
- 4 tablespoons extra-virgin olive oil
- 1 onion, finely chopped
- 3 garlic cloves, minced
- ¼ cup basil, cut into strips
  Direction
- Bring a large pot of water to a boil and cook the pasta according to the package instructions.
- In the last 5 minutes of cooking the pasta, add the shrimp to the hot water and allow them to cook for 3 to 5 minutes. Once they turn pink, take them out of the hot water, and, if you think you may have overcooked them, run them under cool water. Set aside.
- Reserve 1 cup of the pasta cooking water and drain the noodles. In the same pan, heat the oil over medium-high heat and cook the onion and garlic for 7 to 10 minutes. Once the onion is translucent, add the pasta back in and toss well.
- Plate the pasta, then top with shrimp and garnish with basil.
  Nutritional Value: calories: 668 | fat: 19g | protein: 57g | carbohydrates: 73g | fiber: 31g | sodium: 615mg

Fish Tacos

Preparation Time: 40 minutes
Cooking Time: 15 minutes

Servings: 8

Ingredients:

- 1 cup flour
- 2 tablespoons corn flour
- 1 teaspoon baking powder
- 1/2 teaspoon of salt
- 1 egg
- 1 cup of beer
- 1/2 cup of yogurt
- 1/2 cup of mayonnaise
- 1 lime, juice
- 1 jalapeño pepper, minced
- 1 c. Finely chopped capers
- 1/2 teaspoon dried oregano
- 1/2 teaspoon ground cumin
- 1/2 teaspoon dried dill
- 1 teaspoon ground cayenne pepper
- 1 liter of oil for frying
- 1 pound of cod fillets, 2-3 ounces each
- 8 corn tortillas
- 1/2 medium cabbage, finely shredded

Directions:

- Prepare beer dough: combine flour, corn flour, baking powder and salt in a large bowl. Mix the egg and the beer and stir in the flour mixture quickly.
- To make a white sauce: combine yogurt and mayonnaise in a medium bowl. Gradually add fresh lime juice until it is slightly fluid — season with jalapeño, capers, oregano, cumin, dill, and cayenne pepper.
- Heat the oil in a frying pan.
- Lightly sprinkle the fish with flour. Dip it in the beer batter and fry until crispy and golden brown. Drain on kitchen paper. Heat the tortillas. Place the fried fish in a tortilla and garnish with grated cabbage and white sauce.
- Nutrition: 409 calories 18.8 g of fat 43 grams of carbohydrates 17.3 g of protein 54 mg cholesterol 407 mg of sodium.

Grilled Tilapia with Mango Salsa

Preparation Time: 45 minutes
Cooking Time: 10 minutes

Servings: 2

Ingredients:

- 1/3 cup extra virgin olive oil
- 1 tablespoon lemon juice
- 1 tablespoon chopped fresh parsley
- 1 clove of garlic, minced
- 1 teaspoon dried basil
- 1 teaspoon ground black pepper
- 1/2 teaspoon salt
- 2 tilapia fillets (1 oz. each)
- 1 large ripe mango, peeled, pitted and diced
- 1/2 red pepper, diced
- 2 tablespoons chopped red onion
- 1 tablespoon chopped fresh coriander
- 1 jalapeño pepper, seeded and minced
- 2 tablespoons lime juice
- 1 tablespoon lemon juice
- salt and pepper to taste

Directions

- Mix extra virgin olive oil, 1 tablespoon lemon juice, parsley, garlic, basil, 1 teaspoon pepper, and 1/2 teaspoon salt in a bowl, then pour into a resealable plastic bag. Add the tilapia fillets, cover with the marinade, remove excess air, and close the bag. Marinate in the fridge for 1 hour.
- Prepare the mango salsa by combining the mango, red pepper, red onion, coriander, and jalapeño pepper in a bowl. Add the lime juice and 1 tablespoon lemon juice and mix well. Season with salt and pepper and keep until serving.
- Preheat a grill over medium heat and lightly oil.
- Remove the tilapia from the marinade and remove the excess. Discard the rest of the marinade. Grill the fillets until the fish is no longer translucent in the middle and flake easily with the fork for 3 to 4 minutes on each side, depending on the thickness of the fillets. Serve the tilapia topped with mango salsa.

Nutritional Value: 634 calories 40.2 grams of fat 33.4 g carbohydrates 36.3 g of protein 62 mg cholesterol 697 mg of sodium.

DESSERT RECIPES

Almond Cookies

Preparation Time: 5 minutes
Cooking Time: 10 minutes
Servings: 4-6
Ingredients:

- ½ cup sugar
- 8 tablespoons (1 stick) room temperature salted butter
- 1 large egg
- 1½ cups all-purpose flour
- 1 cup ground almonds or almond flour

Directions:

- Preheat the oven to 375°F. Using a mixer, cream together the sugar and butter. Add the egg and mix until combined.
- Alternately add the flour and ground almonds, ½ cup at a time, while the mixer is on slow.
- Once everything is combined, line a baking sheet with parchment paper. Drop a tablespoon of dough on the baking sheet, keeping the cookies at least 2 inches apart.
- Put the single baking sheet in the oven and bake just until the cookies start to turn brown around the edges for about 5 to 7 minutes.
Nutritional Value: Calories 604 Fat 36g Carbs 63g Protein 11g

Crunchy Sesame Cookies

Preparation Time: 10 minutes
Cooking Time: 15 minutes
Servings: 14-16
Ingredients:

- 1 cup sesame seeds, hulled
- 1 cup sugar
- 8 tablespoons (1 stick) salted butter, softened
- 2 large eggs
- 1¼ cups flour

Directions

- Preheat the oven to 350°F. Toast the sesame seeds on a baking sheet for 3 minutes. Set aside and let cool.

- Using a mixer, cream together the sugar and butter. Put the eggs one at a time until well-blended. Add the flour and toasted sesame seeds and mix until well-blended.
- Drop spoonful of cookie dough onto a baking sheet and form them into round balls, about 1-inch in diameter, similar to a walnut.
- Put in the oven and bake for 5 to 7 minutes or until golden brown. Let the cookies cool and enjoy.

Nutritional Value: Calories 218 Fat 12g Carbs 25g Protein 4g

Mini Orange Tarts

Preparation Time: 45 minutes
Cooking Time: 0 minutes
Servings: 2
Ingredients

- 1 cup coconut flour
- 1/2 cup almond flour
- A pinch of grated nutmeg
- A pinch of sea salt
- 1/4 teaspoon ground cloves
- 1/4 teaspoon ground anise
- 1 cup brown sugar
- 6 eggs
- 2 cups heavy cream
- 2 oranges, peeled and sliced

Directions

- Begin by preheating your oven to 350 degrees F.
- Thoroughly combine the flour with spices. Stir in the sugar, eggs, and heavy cream. Mix again to combine well.
- Divide the batter into six lightly greased ramekins.
- Top with the oranges and bake in the preheated oven for about 40 minutes until the clafoutis is just set. Bon appétit!

Nutritional Value: Calories: 398; Fat: 28.5g; Carbs: 24.9g; Protein: 11.9g

Traditional Kalo Prama

Preparation Time: 45 minutes
Cooking Time: 0 minutes
Servings: 2
Ingredients:

- 2 large eggs
- 1/2 cup Greek yogurt
- 1/2 cup coconut oil
- 1/2 cup sugar
- 8 ounces semolina
- 1 teaspoon baking soda
- 2 tablespoons walnuts, chopped
- 1/4 teaspoon ground nutmeg
- 1/4 teaspoon ground anise
- 1/2 teaspoon ground cinnamon
- 1 cup water
- 1 ½ cups caster sugar
- 1 teaspoon lemon zest
- 1 teaspoon lemon juice

  Directions
- Thoroughly combine the eggs, yogurt, coconut oil, and sugar. Add in the semolina, baking soda, walnuts, nutmeg, anise, and cinnamon.
- Let it rest for 1 ½ hour.
- Bake in the preheated oven at 350 degrees F for approximately 40 minutes or until a tester inserted in the center of the cake comes out dry and clean.
- Transfer to a wire rack to cool completely before slicing.
- Meanwhile, bring the water and caster sugar to a full boil; add in the lemon zest and lemon juice, and turn the heat to a simmer; let it simmer for about 8 minutes or until the sauce has thickened slightly.
- Cut the cake into diamonds and pour the syrup over the top; allow it to soak for about 2 hours. Bon appétit!

  Nutritional Value: Calories: 478; Fat: 22.5g; Carbs: 62.4g; Protein: 8.2g

Turkish-Style Chocolate Halva

Preparation Time: 20 minutes

Cooking Time: 0 minutes

Servings: 2

Ingredients

- 1/2 cup water
- 2 cups sugar
- 2 cups tahini
- 1/4 teaspoon cardamom

- 1/4 teaspoon cinnamon
- A pinch of sea salt
- 6 ounces dark chocolate, broken into chunks

Directions

- Bring the water to a full boil in a small saucepan. Add in the sugar and stir. Let it cook, stirring occasionally, until a candy thermometer registers 250 degrees F. Heat off.
- Stir in the tahini. Continue to stir with a wooden spoon just until halva comes together in a smooth mass; do not overmix your halva.
- Add in the cardamom, cinnamon, and salt; stir again to combine well. Now, scrape your halva into a parchment-lined square pan.
- Microwave the chocolate until melted; pour the melted chocolate over your halva and smooth the top.
- Let it cool to room temperature; cover tightly with a plastic wrap and place in your refrigerator for at least 2 hours. Bon appétit!

Nutritional Value: Calories: 388; Fat: 27.5g; Carbs: 31.6g; Protein: 7.9g

SPECIAL RECIPES IN 15 MINUTES

Beef and Broccoli Stir-Fry

Preparation Time: 20 minutes
Cooking Time: 15 minutes
Servings: 4
Ingredients:

- 1/4 cup soy sauce
- 1 tablespoon sesame oil
- 1 teaspoon garlic chili paste
- 1 pound beef sirloin
- 2 tablespoons almond flour
- 2 tablespoons coconut oil
- 2 cups chopped broccoli florets
- 1 tablespoon grated ginger
- 3 cloves garlic, minced
Directions:
- In a small bowl, whisk the soy sauce, sesame oil, and chili paste together.
- In a plastic freezer bag, slice the beef and mix with the almond flour.
- Pour in the sauce and toss to coat for 20 minutes, then let rest.
- Heat up the oil over medium to high heat in a large skillet.
- In the pan, add the beef and sauce and cook until the beef is browned.
- Move the beef to the skillet sides, and then add the broccoli, ginger, and garlic.
- Sauté until tender-crisp broccoli, then throw it all together and serve hot.
Nutritional Value: 350 calories, 19 g fat, 37.5 g protein, 6.5 g carbs, 2 g fiber, 4.5 g net carbs

Parmesan-Crusted Halibut with Asparagus

Preparation Time: 10 minutes
Cooking Time: 15 minutes
Servings: 4
Ingredients:

- 2 tablespoons olive oil
- 1/4 cup butter, softened
- Salt and pepper
- 1/4 cup grated Parmesan

- 1 pound asparagus, trimmed
- 2 tablespoons almond flour
- 4 (6-ounce) boneless halibut fillets
- 1 teaspoon garlic powder

Directions:

- Preheat the oven to 400 F and line a foil-based baking sheet.
- Throw the asparagus in olive oil and scatter over the baking sheet.
- In a blender, add the butter, Parmesan cheese, almond flour, garlic powder, salt and pepper, and mix until smooth.
- Place the fillets with the asparagus on the baking sheet, and spoon the Parmesan over the eggs.
- Bake for 10 to 12 minutes, and then broil until browned for 2 to 3 minutes.

Nutritional Value: 415 calories, 26 g of fat, 42 g of protein, 6 g of carbohydrates, 3 g of fiber, 3 g of net carbs

Hearty Beef and Bacon Casserole

Preparation Time: 25 minutes

Cooking Time: 30 minutes

Servings: 8

Ingredients:

- 8 slices uncooked bacon
- 1 medium head cauliflower, chopped
- ¼ cup canned coconut milk
- Salt and pepper
- 2 pounds ground beef (80% lean)
- 8 ounces mushrooms, sliced
- 1 large yellow onion, chopped
- 2 cloves garlic, minced

Directions:

- Preheat to 375 F on the oven.
- Cook the bacon in a skillet until its crispness, then drain and chop on paper towels.
- Bring to boil a pot of salted water, and then add the cauliflower.
- Boil until tender for 6 to 8 minutes then drain and add the coconut milk to a food processor.
- Mix until smooth, then sprinkle with salt and pepper.
- Cook the beef until browned in a pan, and then wash the fat away.
- Remove the mushrooms, onion, and garlic, and then move to a baking platter.

- Place on top of the cauliflower mixture and bake for 30 minutes.
- Broil for 5 minutes on high heat, then sprinkle with bacon to serve.
  Nutritional Value: 410 calories, 25.5 g of fat, 37 g of protein, 7.5 g of carbohydrates, 3 g of fiber, 4.5 g of net carbs

Sesame Wings with Cauliflower
Preparation Time: 5 minutes
Cooking Time: 30 minutes
Servings: 4
Ingredients:
- 2½ tablespoons soy sauce
- 2 tablespoons sesame oil
- 1½ teaspoons balsamic vinegar
- 1 teaspoon minced garlic
- 1 teaspoon grated ginger
- Salt
- 1-pound chicken wing, the wings itself
- 2 cups cauliflower florets
  Directions
- In a freezer bag, mix the soy sauce, sesame oil, balsamic vinegar, garlic, ginger, and salt, then add the chicken wings.
- Coat flip, and then chill for 2 to 3 hours.
- Preheat the oven to 400 F and line a foil-based baking sheet.
- Spread the wings along with the cauliflower onto the baking sheet.
- Bake for 35 minutes, and then sprinkle on to serve with sesame seeds.
  Nutritional Value: 400 calories, 28.5 g of fat, 31.5 g of protein, 4 g of carbohydrates, 1.5 g of fiber, 2.5 g of carbs

Baked Zucchini Noodles with Feta

Preparation Time: 15 minutes
Cooking Time: 15 minutes
Servings: 1
Ingredients:
- Quartered plum tomato 1
- Spiralized zucchini 2
- Feta cheese 8 cubes
- Pepper 1 tsp.
- Olive oil 1 tbsp.

Directions:

- Set the oven temperature to reach 375° Fahrenheit.
- Slice the noodles with a spiralizer and put the olive oil, tomatoes, pepper, and salt.
- Bake within 10 to 15 minutes. Transfer then put cheese cubes, toss. Serve.
  Nutritional Value: Carbohydrates: 5 grams Protein: 4 grams Total Fats: 8 grams
  Calories: 105

SPECIAL VEGAN RECIPES

Garlic Mushrooms

Preparation Time: 10 minutes
Cooking Time: 15 minutes
Servings: 2

Ingredients:

- 8 oz. mushrooms, rinsed, dried and sliced in half
- 1 tablespoon olive oil
- ½ teaspoon garlic powder
- 1 teaspoon Worcestershire sauce
- 1 tablespoon parsley, chopped

Direction:

- Toss mushrooms in oil.
- Season with garlic powder, salt, pepper and Worcestershire sauce.
- Cook at 380F for 11 minutes, shaking halfway through.
- Top with parsley before serving.

Nutritional Value: Calories 90 Fat 7.4g Protein 3.8g

Rosemary Potatoes

Preparation Time: 15 minutes
Cooking Time: 15 minutes
Servings: 4

Ingredients:

- 4 potatoes, cubed
- 1 tablespoon garlic, minced
- 2 teaspoons dried rosemary, minced
- 1 tablespoon lime juice
- ¼ cup parsley, chopped

Direction

- Toss potato cubes in oil and season with garlic, rosemary, salt and pepper.
- Put in the air fryer.
- Cook at 400F for 15 minutes.
- Stir in lime juice and top with parsley before serving.

Nutritional Value: Calories 244 Fat 10.5g Protein 3.9g

Roasted Spicy Carrots

Preparation Time: 5 minutes
Cooking Time: 15 minutes
Servings: 4
Ingredients:

- ½ lb. carrots, sliced
- ½ tablespoon olive oil
- 1/8 teaspoon garlic powder
- ¼ teaspoon chili powder
- 1 teaspoon ground cumin

Direction

- Prep your air fryer at 390F for 5 minutes.
- Cook the carrots at 390 degrees F for 10 minutes.
- Transfer to a bowl.
- Mix the oil, salt, garlic powder, chili powder and ground cumin.
- Coat the carrots with the oil mixture.
- Put the carrots back to the air fryer and cook for another 5 minutes.
- Garnish with sesame seeds and cilantro.

Nutrition Value: Calories 82 Fat 3.8g Protein 1.2g

Baked Artichoke Fries

Preparation Time: 10 minutes
Cooking Time: 10 minutes
Servings: 4
Ingredients:

- 14 oz. canned artichoke hearts, drained, rinsed and sliced into wedges
- 1 cup all-purpose flour
- ½ cup almond milk
- ½ teaspoon garlic powder; paprika
- 1 ½ cup breadcrumbs

Direction

- Dry the artichoke hearts by pressing a paper towel on top.
- In a bowl, mix the flour, milk, garlic powder, salt and pepper.
- In a shallow dish, add the paprika and breadcrumbs.
- Dip each artichoke wedge in the first bowl and then coat with the breadcrumb mixture.
- Cook at 450 degrees for 10 minutes.
- Serve fries with your choice of dipping sauce.

Nutritional Value: Calories 391 Fat 9.8g Protein 12.7g

Baked Tofu Strips

Preparation Time: 30 minutes
Cooking Time: 40 minutes
Servings: 4
Ingredients:

- 2 tablespoons olive oil
- ½ teaspoon basil; oregano
- ¼ teaspoon cayenne pepper; paprika
- ¼ teaspoon garlic powder; onion powder
- 15 oz. tofu, drained

Direction

- Combine all the ingredients except the tofu.
- Mix well.
- Slice tofu into strips and dry with paper towel.
- Marinate in the mixture for 10 minutes.
- Situate in the air fryer at 375F for 15 minutes, shaking halfway through.

Nutritional Value: Calories 132 Fat 10g Protein 7g

SPECIAL VEGETARIAN RECIPES

Lemon Broccoli Rabe

Preparation Time: 10 minutes
Cooking Time: 10 minutes
Servings: 4

Ingredients:

- 8 cups water
- Sea salt to taste
- 2 bunches broccoli rabe, chopped
- 3 tablespoons olive oil
- 3 garlic cloves, minced
- Pinch of cayenne pepper
- Zest of 1 lemon

Directions

- Boil 8 cups of water. Sprinkle a pinch of salt and the broccoli rabe. Cook until the broccoli rabe is slightly softened, about 2 minutes. Drain.
- Heat olive oil over medium-high heat. Cook the garlic for 30 seconds. Stir in the broccoli rabe, cayenne, and lemon zest. Season with salt and black pepper. Serve immediately.
Nutritional Value: 99 Calories 7g Fiber 11g Protein

Spicy Swiss Chard

Preparation Time: 10 minutes
Cooking Time: 10 minutes
Servings: 4

Ingredients:

- 2 tablespoons olive oil
- 1 onion, chopped
- 2 bunches Swiss chard
- 3 garlic cloves, minced
- ½ teaspoon red pepper flakes (or to taste)
- Juice of ½ lemon

Directions

- In a big pot, cook olive oil over medium-high heat until it shimmers. Cook the onion and chard stems for 5 minutes.
- Cook chard leaves for 1 minute. Stir in the garlic and pepper flakes. Cover and cook for 5 minutes. Stir in the lemon juice. Season with salt and serve immediately.

Nutritional Value: 94 Calories 5g Fiber 7g Protein

Roasted Almond Protein Salad

Preparation Time: 30 minutes

Cooking Time: 0 minutes

Servings: 4

Ingredients:

- ½ cup dry quinoa
- ½ cup dry navy beans
- ½ cup dry chickpeas
- ½ cup raw whole almonds
- 1 teaspoon extra-virgin olive oil
- ½ teaspoon salt
- ½ teaspoon paprika
- ½ teaspoon cayenne
- Dash of chili powder
- 4 cups spinach, fresh or frozen
- ¼ cup purple onion, chopped

Directions

- Prepare the quinoa according to the recipe. Store in the fridge for now.
- Prepare the beans according to the method. Store in the fridge for now.
- Toss the almonds, olive oil, salt, and spices in a large bowl, and stir until the ingredients are evenly coated.
- Put a skillet over medium-high heat, and transfer the almond mixture to the heated skillet.
- Roast while stirring until the almonds are browned, around 5 minutes. You may hear the ingredients pop and crackle in the pan as they warm up. Stir frequently to prevent burning.
- Turn off the heat and toss the cooked and chilled quinoa and beans, onions, spinach, or mixed greens in the skillet. Stir well before transferring the roasted almond salad to a bowl.
- Enjoy the salad with a dressing of choice, or, store for later!
  Nutritional Value: Calories 347 Total Fat 10.5g Saturated Fat 1g Cholesterol 0mg Sodium 324mg Total Carbohydrate 49.2g Dietary Fiber 14.7g Total Sugars 4.7g Protein 17.2g Vitamin D 0mcg Calcium 139mg Iron 5mg Potassium 924mg

Black-Eyed Pea, Beet, and Carrot Stew

Preparation Time: 15 minutes

Cooking Time: 40 minutes

Servings: 2

Ingredients:

- ½ cup black-eyed peas, soaked in water overnight
- 3 cups water
- 1 large beet, peeled and cut into ½-inch pieces (about ¾ cup)
- 1 large carrot, peeled and cut into ½-inch pieces (about ¾ cup)
- ¼ teaspoon turmeric
- ¼ teaspoon toasted and ground cumin seeds
- 1/8 teaspoon asafetida
- ¼ cup finely chopped parsley
- ¼ teaspoon cayenne pepper
- ¼ teaspoon salt (optional)
- ½ teaspoon fresh lime juice

Directions

Pour the black-eyed peas and water into a pot, then cook over medium heat for 25 minutes.

Add the beet and carrot to the pot and cook for 10 more minutes. Add more water if necessary.

Add the turmeric, cumin, asafetida, parsley, and cayenne pepper to the pot and cook for an additional 6 minutes or until the vegetables are soft. Stir the mixture periodically.

Sprinkle with salt, if desired.

Drizzle the lime juice on top before serving in a large bowl.

Nutrition Value: calories: 84 | fat: 0.7g | carbs: 16.6g | protein: 4.1g | fiber: 4.5g

Koshari

Preparation Time: 15 minutes

Cooking Time: 2 hours 10 minutes

Servings: 6

Ingredients:

- 1 cup green lentils, rinsed
- 3 cups water
- Salt, to taste (optional)
- 1 large onion, peeled and minced
- 2 tablespoons low-sodium vegetable broth
- 4 cloves garlic, peeled and minced

- ½ teaspoon ground allspice
- 1 teaspoon ground coriander
- 1 teaspoon ground cumin
- 2 tablespoons tomato paste
- ½ teaspoon crushed red pepper flakes
- 3 large tomatoes, diced
- 1 cup cooked medium-grain brown rice
- 1 cup whole-grain elbow macaroni, cooked, drained, and kept warm
- 1 tablespoon brown rice vinegar

Directions

- Put the lentils and water in a saucepan, and sprinkle with salt, if desired. Bring to a boil over high heat. Reduce the heat to medium, then put the pan lid on and cook for 45 minutes or until the water is mostly absorbed. Pour the cooked lentils into the bowl and set aside.
- Add the onion to a nonstick skillet, then sauté over medium heat for 15 minutes or caramelized.
- Add vegetable broth and garlic to the skillet and sauté for 3 minutes or until fragrant.
- Add the allspice, coriander, cumin, tomato paste, and red pepper flakes to the skillet and sauté for an additional 3 minutes until aromatic.
- Add the tomatoes to the skillet and sauté for 15 minutes or until the tomatoes are wilted. Sprinkle with salt, if desired.
- Arrange the cooked brown rice on the bottom of a large platter, then top the rice with macaroni, and then spread the lentils over. Pour the tomato mixture and brown rice vinegar over before serving.

Nutritional Value: Calories: 201 Fat: 1.6g Carbs: 41.8g Protein: 6.5g Fiber: 3

SPECIAL GLUTEN RECIPES

Blueberries Quinoa

Preparation Time: 5 minutes
Cooking Time: 0 minutes
Servings: 4
Ingredients:

- 2 cups quinoa, almond milk
- ½ teaspoon cinnamon powder
- 1 tablespoon honey
- 1 cup blueberries
- ¼ cup walnuts, chopped

Directions:

- In a bowl, scourge quinoa with the milk and the rest of the ingredients, toss, divide into smaller bowls and serve for breakfast.
Nutritional Value: 284 calories 14.3g fat 4.4g protein

Raspberries and Yogurt Smoothie

Preparation Time: 5 minutes
Cooking Time: 0 minutes
Servings: 2
Ingredients:

- 2 cups raspberries
- ½ cup Greek yogurt
- ½ cup almond milk
- ½ teaspoon vanilla extract

Directions:

- In your blender, combine the raspberries with the milk, vanilla and the yogurt, pulse well, divide into 2 glasses and serve for breakfast.
Nutritional Value: 245 calories 9.5g fat 1.6g protein

Cottage Cheese and Berries Omelet

Preparation Time: 5 minutes
Cooking Time: 4 minutes
Servings: 1
Ingredients:

- 1 egg, whisked
- 1 teaspoon cinnamon powder
- 1 tablespoon almond milk
- 3 ounces cottage cheese
- 4 ounces blueberries

Directions:

- Scourge egg with the rest of the ingredients except the oil and toss.
- Preheat pan with the oil over medium heat, add the eggs mix, spread, cook for 4 minutes on both sides, then serve.

Nutritional Value: 190 calories8g fat2g protein

Salmon Frittata

Preparation Time: 5 minutes

Cooking Time: 27 minutes

Servings: 4

Ingredients:

- 1-pound gold potatoes, roughly cubed
- 1 tablespoon olive oil
- 2 salmon fillets, skinless and boneless
- 8 eggs, whisked
- 1 teaspoon mint, chopped

Directions:

- Put the potatoes in a boiling water at medium heat, then cook for 12 minutes, drain and transfer to a bowl.
- Spread the salmon on a baking sheet lined with parchment paper, grease with cooking spray, broil at medium-high heat for 10 minutes on both sides, cool down, flake and put in a separate bowl.
- Warm up a pan with the oil over medium heat, add the potatoes, salmon, and the rest of the ingredients excluding the eggs and toss.
- Add the eggs on top, put the lid on and cook over medium heat for 10 minutes.
- Divide the salmon between plates and serve.

Nutritional Value: 289 calories 11g fat 4g protein

Avocado and Olive Paste on Toasted Rye Bread

Preparation Time: 5 minutes

Cooking Time: 0 minute

Servings: 4

Ingredients:
- 1 avocado, halved, peeled and finely chopped
- 1 tbsp. green onions, finely chopped
- 2 tbsp. green olive paste
- 4 lettuce leaves
- 1 tbsp. lemon juice
Directions:
- Crush avocados with a fork or potato masher until almost smooth. Add the onions, green olive paste and lemon juice. Season with salt and pepper to taste. Stir to combine.
- Toast 4 slices of rye bread until golden. Spoon 1/4 of the avocado mixture onto each slice of bread, top with a lettuce leaf and serve.

Nutritional Value: 291 calories 13g fat 3g protein

SALAD

Brown Rice Salad with Pistachios and Basil

Preparation Time: 5 Minutes

Cooking Time: 30 Minutes

Servings: 6 to 8

Ingredients:

- One can (15-ounces) chickpeas, drained, rinsed
- 1 cup brown rice, uncooked long-grain
- One medium red bell pepper, cored
- One small red onion, finely diced
- One teaspoon red chili flake, crushed
- One teaspoon kosher, or more to taste (or fine sea salt)
- 1/2 cup fresh basil leaves, definitely packed, cut into thin strips (chiffonade)
- 1/2 cup golden raisins
- 1/2 cup pistachio nuts, raw unsalted
- 1/4 cup plus two tablespoons mild-tasting olive oil
- 1/4 cup red wine vinegar
- Four medium-large cloves garlic, finely diced

Directions:

- Fill a medium-sized pan with water; bring to a boil over high heat. Add the rice; return to a boil. Cook with the lid open for about 20-25 minutes or until the riced are cooked, tender, but still a bit chewy. Drain the rice using a sieve and rinse under running cold water to stop cooking; set aside
- When the rice is cooking, put the raisins, vinegar, and 1/4 cup of the olive oil in a blender, process until smooth vinaigrette, scraping the sides of the jar if needed.
- Over medium-high heat, heat a 10-inch skillet. Add the pistachios; toast for about 2 minutes, frequently stirring until some brown and fragrant spots with a strong nutty aroma. Move the toasted nuts to a cutting board. When cool enough to handle, chop coarsely.
- In the same skillet, heat the lasting two tablespoons olive oil over medium-high heat until very hot. Stir fry the garlic and the onion for about 2-3 minutes, or until honey brown; scrape into a large-sized bowl. Add the pistachios, chickpeas, vinaigrette, bell pepper, red chili flakes, and salt. Add the rice; fold the ingredients.
- Just before serving, fold in the basil. Taste and season with salt, if desired.

Nutrition Value: Cal 330 Fat 15g Protein 8g Carb 41g

Spinach and Avocado Salad

Preparation Time: 5 Minutes

Cooking Time: 0 Minutes

Servings: 4

Ingredients:

- Two tablespoons olive oil
- Three tablespoons balsamic vinegar
- One teaspoon basil, dried
- Three avocados, peeled, pitted, and cubed
- 2 cups baby spinach
- Salt and black pepper to the taste
- One small red onion, chopped
- One tablespoon dill, chopped

Directions:

- In a bowl, blend the avocados with the spinach, basil, and the rest of the ingredients, toss and serve right away.

Nutritional Value: Calories 53 Fat 0.3 Fiber 0.5 Carbs 11 Protein 1

Mixed Salad with Balsamic Honey Dressing

Preparation Time: 15 Minutes

Cooking Time: 0 Minutes

Servings: 2

Ingredients:

Dressing:

- ¼ cup balsamic vinegar
- ¼ cup olive oil
- One tablespoon honey
- One teaspoon Dijon mustard
- ¼ teaspoon garlic powder
- ¼ teaspoon salt, or more to taste
- Pinch freshly ground black pepper

Salad:

- 4 cups chopped red leaf lettuce
- ½ cup cherry or grape tomatoes halved
- ½ English cucumber, sliced in quarters lengthwise and then cut into bite-size pieces
- Any combination of fresh, torn herbs (parsley, oregano, basil, or chives)
- One tablespoon roasted sunflower seeds

Directions:

Make the Dressing

- Combine the vinegar, olive oil, honey, mustard, garlic powder, salt, and pepper in a jar with a lid. Shake well.

Make the Salad

- In a bowl, combine the lettuce, tomatoes, cucumber, and herbs. Toss well.
- Pour all or as much dressing as desired over the tossed salad. Toss it again to coat the salad dressing.
- Top with the sunflower seeds before serving.
  Nutritional Value: Calories: 337 Fat: 26.1g Protein: 4.2g Carbs: 22.2g Fiber: 3.1g Sodium: 172mg

Arugula and Fig Salad

Preparation Time: 15 Minutes

Cooking Time: 0 Minutes

Servings: 2

Ingredients:

- 3 cups arugula
- Four fresh, ripe figs (or 4 to 6 dried figs), stemmed and sliced
- Two tablespoons olive oil
- ¼ cup lightly toasted pecan halves
- Two tablespoons crumbled blue cheese
- 1 to 2 tablespoons balsamic glaze

Directions:

- Toss the arugula and figs with the olive oil in a large bowl until evenly coated.
- Add the pecans and blue cheese to the bowl. Toss the salad lightly.
- Drizzle with the balsamic glaze and serve immediately.
  Nutritional Value: Calories: 517 Fat: 36.2g Protein: 18.9g Carbs: 30.2g Fiber: 6.1g Sodium: 481mg

Arugula, Watermelon, and Feta Salad

Preparation Time: 10 Minutes

Cooking Time: 0 Minutes

Servings: 2

Ingredients:

- 3 cups packed arugula
- 2½ cups watermelon, cut into bite-size cubes

- 2 ounces (57 g) feta cheese, crumbled
- Two tablespoons balsamic glaze

Directions:

- Divide the arugula between two plates.
- Divide the watermelon cubes between the beds of arugula.
- Scatter half of the feta cheese over each salad.
- Drizzle about one tablespoon of the glaze (or more if desired) over each salad. Serve immediately.

Nutritional Value: Calories: 157 Fat: 6.9g Protein: 6.1g Carbs: 22.0g Fiber: 1.1gSodium: 328mg

Green Bean and Halloumi Salad

Preparation Time: 20 Minutes

Cooking Time: 5 Minutes

Servings: 2

Ingredients:

Dressing:

- ¼ cup unsweetened coconut milk
- One tablespoon olive oil
- Two teaspoons freshly squeezed lemon juice
- ¼ teaspoon garlic powder
- ¼ teaspoon onion powder
- Pinch salt
- Pinch freshly ground black pepper

Salad:

- ½ pound (227 g) fresh green beans, trimmed
- 2 ounces (57 g) Halloumi cheese, sliced into 2 (½-inch-thick) slices
- ½ cup halved cherry or grape tomatoes
- ¼ cup thinly sliced sweet onion

Directions:

Make the Dressing

- Combine the coconut milk, olive oil, lemon juice, onion powder, garlic powder, salt, and pepper in a small bowl and whisk well. Set aside.

Make the Salad

- Fill a medium-size pot with about 1 inch of water and add the green beans. Cover and steam them for about 3 to 4 minutes, or just until beans are tender. Do not overcook. Drain beans, rinse them immediately with cold water and set them aside to cool.

- Heat a nonstick skillet over medium-high heat and place the slices of Halloumi in the hot pan. After around 2 minutes, check to see if the cheese is golden on the bottom. If it is, flip the slices and cook for another minute or until the second side is golden.
- Remove cheese from the pan and cut each piece into cubes (about 1-inch square).
- Place the green beans, halloumi slices, tomatoes, and onion in a large bowl and toss to combine.
- Sprinkle the dressing over the salad and pitch well to combine. Serve immediately. Nutrition: Calories: 274 Fat: 18.1g Protein: 8.0gCarbs: 16.8g Fiber: 5.1gSodium: 499mg

Citrus Salad with Kale and Fennel

Preparation Time: 15 Minutes

Cooking Time: 0 Minutes

Servings: 2

Ingredients:

Dressing:

- Three tablespoons olive oil
- Two tablespoons fresh orange juice
- One tablespoon blood orange vinegar, other orange vinegar, or cider vinegar
- One tablespoon honey
- Salt and freshly ground black pepper

Salad:

- 2 cups packed baby kale
- One medium navel or blood orange, segmented
- ½ small fennel bulb, stems and leaves removed, sliced into matchsticks
- Three tablespoons toasted pecans, chopped
- 2 ounces (57 g) goat cheese, crumbled

Directions:

Make the Dressing

- Mix the olive oil, orange juice, vinegar, and honey in a small bowl and whisk to combine. Season with salt and pepper to taste. Set aside.

Make the Salad

- Divide the baby kale, orange segments, fennel, pecans, and goat cheese evenly between two plates.
- Sprinkle half of the dressing over each salad, and serve.
Nutritional Value: Calories: 503 Fat: 39.1g Protein: 13.2g Carbs: 31.2g Fiber: 6.1g Sodium: 156mg

Cauliflower Tabbouleh Salad

Preparation Time: 15 minutes

Cooking Time: 5 minutes

Servings: 6

Ingredients:

- 6 tablespoons extra-virgin olive oil, divided
- 4 cups riced cauliflower
- 3 garlic cloves, finely minced
- 1½ teaspoons salt
- ½ teaspoon freshly ground black pepper
- ½ large cucumber, peeled, seeded, and chopped
- ½ cup chopped mint leaves
- ½ cup chopped Italian parsley
- ½ cup chopped pitted Kalamata olives
- 2 tablespoons minced red onion
- Juice of 1 lemon (about 2 tablespoons)
- 2 cups baby arugula or spinach leaves
- 2 medium avocados, peeled, pitted, and diced
- 1 cup quartered cherry tomatoes

Directions

- In a broad skillet over medium-high heat, heat 2 tablespoons olive oil. Add the rice cauliflower, garlic, salt, and pepper and sauté until just tender but not mushy, 3 to 4 minutes. Turn off the heat and transfer to a large mixing bowl.
- Add the cucumber, mint, parsley, olives, red onion, lemon juice, and remaining 4 tablespoons olive oil and toss well. Place in the refrigerator, uncovered, and refrigerate for at least 30 minutes, or up to 2 hours.
- Before serving, add the arugula, avocado, and tomatoes and toss to combine well. Season to taste with salt and pepper and serve cold or at room temperature.

Nutritional Value: Calories: 235 Fat: 21 g Protein: 4 g

27 DAY PLAN (DETOX-FOOD BALANCE-LOSE WEIGHT)

DAY 1-7 DETOX

DAY	BREAKFAST	LUNCH	DINNER
1	Fruit Smoothie	Mediterranean Pork Kabobs	Garlic Mushrooms
2	Strawberry-Rhubarb Smoothie	Pasta Fagioli	Spicy Swiss Chard
3	Pastry-Less Spanakopita	Spinach Pesto Pasta	Arugula and Fig Salad
4	Pear Mango Smoothie	Shrimp Pizza	Salmon Fritata
5	Chia-Pomegranate Smoothie	Grilled Salmon	Lemon Broccoli Rabe
6	Mediterranean smoothie	Authentic Pasta e Fagioli	Almond Cookies
7	Fruit Smoothie	Cold lemon zoodles	Cauliflower Tabbouleh Salad

DAY 8-21 FOOD BALANCE

DAY	Mango Pear Smoothie	15 Minute Caprese Pasta Recipe	Rosemary Potatoes

8	Fruit Smoothie	Shrimp and Pasta Stew	Fish Tacos
9	Blueberry, Hazlenut, and Lemon Breakfast Grain Salad	Spinach Peso Pasta	Almond cookies
10	Pear Mango Smoothie	Cheese Pinwheels	Baked Tofu Strips
11	Mediterranean Smoothie	Easy Mediterranean Burers	Spicy Swiss Chard
12	Blueberry Greek Yogurt Pancakes	Seafood Paella	Sweet Potatoes Oven Fried
13	Pastry-Less Spanakopita	Garlic Mushrooms	Seafood Paella
14	Date and Walnut Overnight Oats	Pasta Fagioli	Brown Rice Salad with Pistachios and Basil
15	Shrimp Pizza	Cold Lemon Zoodles	Spinash and Avocado Salad
16	Hummus with Spiced Beef Toasted Pine Nuts	Lebanese Meat Pies	Mixed Salad with Balsamic Honey Dressing
17	Mediterranean Smoothie	Mediterranean Pork Chops	Arugula and Fig Salad
18	Fruit Smoothie	Dill Relish on White Sea Bass	Arugula, Watermelon, and Feta Salad
19	Strawberry Rhubarb Smoothie	Almond-Crusted Swordfish	Green Bean and Halloumi Salad

20	Chia-Pomegranate Smoothie	Beef and Broccoli Stir fry	Citrus Salad with Kale and Fennel
21	Feta-Avocado and Mashed Chickpea Toast	Black Bean Pasta	Cauliflower Tabbouleh Salad

DAY 22-27 LOSE WEIGHT

DAY	BREAKFAST	LUNCH	DINNER
22	Egg white Scramble with Cherry Tomatoes & Spinach	Veggie Pizza	Rosemary Potatoes
23	Fruit Smoothie	Za'atar Pizza	Baked Artichoke Fries
24	Pastry-less spanakopita	Lebanese Meat Pies	Koshari
25	Peer Mango Smoothie	Baked Sea Bass	Salmon Fritata
26	Easy Italian Shrimp Tortellini Bake	Crispy Sardines	Beef and Broccoli Stir
27	Date and Walnut Overnight Oats	Spinach Pesto Pasta	Crispy Sardine

CONCLUSION

If you need to do something, it's important to be able to do it well. To get better at things that matter most to us, we can learn and practice. Consuming the Mediterranean diet is known to help with weight loss and other health benefits, but there are also many ways in which people can improve their diet by reading about healthful Mediterranean food options. The following blog post will touch on these points and give suggestions on how readers can enjoy a healthy Mediterranean lifestyle.

There are also many ways that people can improve their lifestyle when following the Mediterranean diet. The following are just a few ideas for those who want to achieve their weight-loss objectives.

The first thing is to pick foods that are more flavorful than you normally would. When reading the Mediterranean diet, many readers might feel compelled to always eat bland meals and snacks that don't contain much flavor. The solution to this problem is to go out and get your hands on some homemade pesto sauce and marinara sauce because both of them contain a lot of flavors but little calories. By adding these sauces to your meals, it will boost the taste without adding extra calories. This way you can still enjoy your healthy food choices and it will taste great, too.

The second thing is to not be afraid to experiment. Many people shy away from trying new foods because they're afraid that they won't like them and will end up eating too much of the same foods over and over again. This happens because these people make their food choices based on what they already like instead of trying something new and trying recipes that look good on the menu. This is why it's so essential to make an effort to sample new foods; don't be scared to try something new every now and again, even if you've already tasted that cuisine.

The next point to remember is that your training routine must be quite strenuous. While being able to get enough exercise is important for overall health, a normal working out routine will work just fine when it comes to the Mediterranean diet. It's very important for people to incorporate some sort of activity into their daily schedule because lack of physical activity increases one's risk for death from all causes during the early years of one's lifespan. This means that if you're not up and about on a regular basis, then chances are you're going to die sooner than you should. The more active you are, the longer your life will be and this is why it's so important not to skip out on your exercises.

The fourth thing that people should remember is not to become obsessed with their weight. Many people find that the first time they start following the Mediterranean diet, they end up weighing themselves very often because they're trying to keep track of how much weight they've lost. It's important for readers to remember that you shouldn't feel like you need to weigh yourself on a daily basis because it can be very frustrating if you gain weight over the weekend and your scale doesn't register the gain until Monday morning. Some scales even incorrectly measure your height so don't put too much emphasis on what your scale says about your weight loss. Instead, focus on how you feel instead of just what you weigh.

The final thing that is worth mentioning is for people to make sure not to confuse the Mediterranean diet with the Japanese diet. These two diets are very different and only share the similarities of them both being healthy. The Japanese diet is full of things like rice, noodles and seafood whereas the Mediterranean diet includes mostly Mediterranean foods such as fruits and vegetables. It's very important for readers to understand that these two diets are quite different and that if they want to try a new way of eating, then they need to be sure that it's by following a Mediterranean diet.

With all of this information available, it should be easy for people to start following the Mediterranean diet in an effort to reap all of its benefits. In fact, it's quite easy to do so because the Mediterranean diet is rich in recipes that everyone will enjoy. This means that if someone wants to try a new way of eating, they can search through a variety of different websites and blogs where they can find a wide array of healthy recipes for various types of foods in addition to one or two simple recipes that you can follow to get started on your diet. This way you'll only have to make a few changes in order to start following this diet.

WOW BONUS

Basic Conversion Charts

weight
(rounded to the nearest whole number)

IMPERIAL	METRIC
0.5 oz	14 g
1 oz	28 g
2 oz	58 g
3 oz	86 g
4 oz	114 g
5 oz	142 g
6 oz	170 g
7 oz	198 g
8 oz (1/2 lb)	226 g
9 oz	256 g
10 oz	284 g
11 oz	312 g
12 oz	340 g
13 oz	368 g
14 oz	396 g
15 oz	426 g
16 oz (1 lb)	454 g
24 oz (1 1/2 lb)	680 g

misc
(rounded to the closest equivalent)

IMPERIAL	
1 quart	4 cups (1 liter)
4 quarts	16 cups (4.5 liters)
6 quarts	24 cups (7 liters)
1 gallon	16 cups (4.5 liters)

volume
(rounded to the closest equivalent)

IMPERIAL	METRIC
1/8 tsp	0.5 mL
1/4 tsp	1 mL
1/2 tsp	2.5 mL
3/4 tsp	4 mL
1 tsp	5 mL
1 tbsp	15 mL
1 1/2 tbsp	25 mL
1/8 cup	30 mL
1/4 cup	60 mL
1/3 cup	80 mL
1/2 cup	120 mL
2/3 cup	160 mL
3/4 cup	180 mL
1 cup	240 mL

liquid
(rounded to the closest equivalent)

IMPERIAL	METRIC
0.5 oz	15 mL
1 oz	30 mL
2 oz	60 mL
3 oz	85 mL
4 oz	115 mL
5 oz	140 mL
6 oz	170 mL
7 oz	200 mL
8 oz	230 mL
9 oz	260 mL
10 oz	285 mL
11 oz	310 mL
12 oz	340 mL
13 oz	370 mL

temperature
(rounded to the closest equivalent)

IMPERIAL	METRIC
150°F	65°C
160°F	70°C
175°F	80°C
200°F	95°C
225°F	110°C
250°F	120°C
275°F	135°C
300°F	150°C
325°F	160°C
350°F	175°C
375°F	190°C
400°F	205°C
425°F	220°C
450°F	230°C
475°F	245°C
500°F	260°C

length
(rounded to the closest equivalent)

IMPERIAL	METRIC
1/8 inch	3 mm
1/4 inch	6 mm
1 inch	2.5 cm
1 1/4 inch	3 cm
2 inches	5 cm
6 inches	15 cm
8 inches	20 cm
9 inches	22.5 cm
10 inches	25 cm
11 inches	28 cm

Cooking Measurement Conversion Chart

QUICK ALTERNATIVES

1	tablespoon (tbsp)	3	teaspoons (tsp)
1/16	cup	1	tablespoon
1/8	cup	2	tablespoons
1/6	cup	2	tablespoons + 2 teaspoons
1/4	cup	4	tablespoons
1/3	cup	5	tablespoons + 1 teaspoon
3/8	cup	6	tablespoons
1/2	cup	8	tablespoons
2/3	cup	10	tablespoons + 2 teaspoons
3/4	cup	12	tablespoons
1	cup	48	teaspoons
1	cup	16	tablespoons
8	fluid ounces (fl oz)	1	cup
1	pint (pt)	2	cups
1	quart (qt)	2	pints
4	cups	1	quart
1	gallon (gal)	4	quarts
16	ounces (oz)	1	pound (lb)
1	milliliter (ml)	1	cubic centimeter (cc)
1	inch (in)	2.54	centimeters (cm)

CAPACITY (U.S to Metric)

1/5 teaspoon	1 milliliter
1 teaspoon	5 ml
1 tablespoon	15 ml
1 fluid oz	30 ml
1/5 cup	47 ml
1 cup	237 ml
2 cups (1 pint)	473 ml
4 cups (1 quart)	.95 liter
4 quarts (1 gal.)	3.8 liters

CAPACITY (Metric to U.S.)

1	milliliter	1/5 teaspoon
5	ml	1 teaspoon
15	ml	1 tablespoon
100	ml	3.4 fluid oz
240	ml	1 cup
1	liter	34 fluid oz
		4.2 cups
		2.1 pints
		1.06 quarts
		0.26 gallon

WEIGHT (U.S to Metric)

1	oz	28 grams
1	pound	454 grams

WEIGHT (Metric to U.S.)

1	gram	0.035 ounce
100	grams	3.5 ounces
500	grams	1.1 pounds
1	kilogram	2.205 pounds
		35 ounces

Printed in Great Britain
by Amazon